International Dimensions of
THE LEGAL ENVIRONMENT
OF BUSINESS

THE KENT INTERNATIONAL DIMENSIONS OF BUSINESS SERIES

International Dimensions of
THE LEGAL ENVIRONMENT
OF BUSINESS

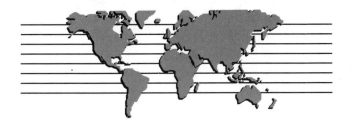

Michael Litka
University of Akron

THE KENT INTERNATIONAL DIMENSIONS OF BUSINESS SERIES
David A. Ricks
Series Consulting Editor

PWS-KENT Publishing Company
Boston, Massachusetts

Editor: Rolf Janke
Assistant Editor: Kathleen M. Tibbetts
Production Editor: Pamela Rockwell
Text Designer: Elise Kaiser
Cover Designer: Julie Gecha
Manufacturing Manager: Ellen Glisker

PWS–KENT
Publishing Company

PWS-KENT Publishing Company is a division of Wadsworth, Inc.

Printed in the United States of America
1 2 3 4 5 6 7 8 9 — 92 91 90 89 88

Library of Congress Cataloging-in-Publication Data

Litka, Michael P.
    International dimensions of the legal environment of business.

(The Kent international dimensions of business series)
Includes bibliographies and index.
    1. Foreign trade regulation.   2. Commercial treaties.
3. Export sales contracts.   4. International business
enterprises — Law and legislation.   I. Title.   II. Series.
K563.B87L58   1988   341.7′54   88–17966
ISBN 0–534–87208–5

Series Foreword

Prior to World War II, the number of firms involved in foreign direct investment was relatively small. Although several U.S. companies were obtaining raw materials from other countries, most firms were interested only in the U.S. market. This situation changed, however, during the 1950s — especially after the creation of the European Economic Community. Since that time, there has been a rapid expansion in international business activity.

The majority of the world's large corporations now perform an increasing proportion of their business activities outside their home countries. For many of these companies, international business returns over one-half of their profits, and it is becoming more and more common for a typical corporation to earn at least one-fourth of its profits through international business involvement. In fact, it is now rather rare for any large firm not to be a participant in the world of international business.

International business is of great importance in most countries, and that importance continues to grow. To meet the demand for increased knowledge in this area, business schools are attempting to add international dimensions to their curricula. Faculty members are becoming more interested in teaching a greater variety of international business courses and are striving to add international dimensions to other courses. Students, aware of the increasing probability that they will be employed by firms engaged in international business activities, are seeking knowledge of the problem-solving techniques unique to international business. As the American Assembly of Collegiate Schools of Business has observed, however, there is a shortage of available information. Most business textbooks do not adequately consider the international dimensions of business, and much of the supplemental material is disjointed, overly narrow, or otherwise inadequate in the classroom.

This series has been developed to overcome such problems. The books are written by some of the most respected authors in the various areas of international business. Each author is extremely well known in the Academy of International Business and in his or her other professional academies. They possess an outstanding knowledge of their own subject matter and a talent for explaining it.

These books, in which the authors have identified the most important international aspects of their fields, have been written in a format that facilitates their use as supplemental material in business school courses. For the most part, the material is presented by topic in approximately the same order and manner as it is covered in basic business textbooks. Therefore, as each topic is covered in the course, material is easily supplemented with the corresponding chapter in the series book.

The Kent International Dimensions of Business Series offers a unique and much-needed opportunity to bring international dimensions of business into the classroom. The series has been developed by leaders in the field after years of discussion and careful consideration, and the timely encouragement and support provided by the PWS-KENT staff on this project. I am proud to be associated with this series and highly recommend it to you.

David A. Ricks

Consulting Editor to the
  Kent International Dimensions of Business Series
Professor of International Business,
  University of South Carolina

Preface

The world trade that began for the United States in the era of the Yankee clipper ship — long since faded — continues to grow. Modern transportation and communication have facilitated the expansion of the international marketplace. Today, exporting and importing are not restricted solely to the movement of goods; nations export and import capital, technology, patents, and any number of services, and people move across and within international borders. The evolution of international trade in its many forms and the resulting charge by the American Assembly of Collegiate Schools of Business to present material on this subject to students are of concern to collegiate schools of business.

An introductory text on the international legal environment of business will necessarily present some type of survey or overview of law. This author has adopted a broad approach so that the student will be able to grasp the whole of the subject while gaining an understanding of some of the basic principles. For example, an investor will have to have a general understanding of the Act of State Doctrine as it applies to the risks of the individual transaction. Likewise, before an investor can properly analyze a particular commercial treaty, he or she must understand that a treaty is a contract between sovereign states that is subject to the vagaries of international law. International expansion is a factor in American business. It is the primary object of *International Dimensions of the Legal Environment of Business* to study the legal problems that arise when business activities and organizations cross national boundaries and become multinational in structure, operation, and scope. As a business moves beyond a single country and extends its operations to more countries, its need for legal awareness grows proportionately. This volume in the International Dimensions series is designed to analyze the primary sources of the legal problems confronting a multinational business venture.

The goal of *International Dimensions of the Legal Environment of Business* is to present in an orderly sequence legal materials that apply to decisions made and implemented in international business. Emphasis is placed on the business enterprise as it conducts its commercial activity in environments that are different in their economic, political, social, and cultural aspects from the firm's corresponding domestic environment. Various aspects of conflicts of law, constitutional law, contracts, sales, finance, insurance, corporations, tax, anti-trust, civil procedure, and administrative law make up the contents of this volume. Specific attention has been paid to the legal effects of international business decisions, the impact of governmental authority, the legal status of treaties and tariffs, and the difficulties of international dispute settlement procedures.

International Dimensions of the Legal Environment of Business is an ambitious undertaking because at present there are no uniformly accepted international norms of business law. That does not mean that there is no international business law recognized by so-called civilized nations. However, it is a body of law in which few decisions have been rendered by international tribunals. The controlling principles, therefore, are the general principles of international law. The field is further complicated by the private law made by parties to international transactions, which involves sales, contracts, financing, and dispute settlement.

International Dimensions of the Legal Environment of Business has been written in order to internationalize courses in business law and also as a core volume that will permit an instructor, through supplements, to develop an independent first course in the international legal environment of business.

I am grateful for the constructive comments made by the reviewers of the manuscript: Mark B. Baker, The University of Texas at Austin; and Carolyn Hotchkiss, Babson College.

Michael Litka

About the Author

Mike Litka is currently Professor of Business Law at the University of Akron, where he developed a course in international business law and serves as a member of the International Business Committee of the College of Business Administration. He received a Master's degree in history and his J.D. from the University of Iowa and has authored several texts on business law and the legal environment of business. He has presented a number of papers on international law to the American Business Law Association, the Midwest Business Law Association, and the Tri-State Business Law Association. In 1985, he received the outstanding paper award as co-author of "Taxation of the Multijurisdictional Corporation." His casebook in international law was published in 1987 and numerous articles have appeared in *The Oil and Gas Quarterly*, *The Midwest Law Review*, and the *Journal of Legal Studies*. Professor Litka is a past president of the American Business Law Association and past president and current executive secretary of the Tri-State Regional Business Law Association.

Contents

CONTENTS

International Dimensions of
THE LEGAL ENVIRONMENT
OF BUSINESS

CHAPTER 1

▼

World Business and International Law: An Overview

▲

Although world trade has been an economic fact for centuries, today the world is in an age of unprecedented economic activity. Opportunity awaits the domestic firm and the individual willing to study and understand the rules of world trade. In fact, many firms earn more in world than in domestic operations. There is little doubt, however, that world trade involves complications not found in domestic transactions. In addition to differences in climate, language, and social, political, and business customs, for example, there are differences in the laws governing commercial transactions.

All countries exert extensive control over trade taking place with other countries, and all countries act in their own self-interest. These facts, perhaps more than any other, distinguish world trade from domestic. Also, trading between government-controlled economies and those dominated by the laws of supply and demand often involves differences. Their rules may be different, and they may have different reasons for trading. Before one can understand these differences or the basic legal principles affecting world trade, an overview of the legal and domestic environment of world trade is necessary. The term *environment* encompasses those factors that influence the life and development of world trade.

THE NATURE OF WORLD BUSINESS

The term *business* includes all the activities of organizations that provide the goods and services that satisfy a state's material needs. The domestic business system operates within geographic constraints, whereas worldwide activities have no fixed territorial boundaries. Sometimes the activity occurs between only two sovereign nations, at other times, between one country and the rest of the world. World business activities include the exporting and importing of goods; exploiting natural resources; direct investment; the licensing of processes, patents, or trademarks; supplying personal services such as marketing, financial, technological, transportation, or managerial expertise; and related activities, such as shipping and insurance.

The Reasons for World Business

In *The Schooner Exchange* v. *McFaddon*, 7 Cranch 116 (1812), Chief Justice Marshall wrote: "The world [is] composed of distinct sovereignties . . . whose mutual benefit is promoted by intercourse with each other, and by an interchange of those good offices which humanity dictates and its wants require. . . ." This observation alludes to a fact of world trade: a mutual benefit in the exchange of goods, or the principle of **comparative advantage.** For example, one nation may be able to produce a good more efficiently than another because of an economic advantage in labor, technology, or raw materials. It will be to its advantage to export that good. The importing nation can, therefore, concentrate on producing other goods more efficiently in order to have them available for export. Thus, each nation will export those goods in which it has an advantage and import those goods in which it has a disadvantage, which results in a degree of interdependence among the economies of the world that will vary among the several nations. For example, for years the American farmer has produced great surpluses, which have been absorbed in part by the foreign market. At the same time, the American steel industry depends on imports of lead, manganese, nickel, tin, and zinc.

Differences Between Domestic and World Business

Domestic Environments

Business organizations may be either privately owned or they may be government enterprises (or a combination of the two). In the case of the private organization, business activities are carried out for profit, whereas government-sponsored activities may or may not be profit motivated. Contrary to the capitalist doctrine of private ownership of the basic means of production, distribution, and exchange, the socialist doctrine advocates government ownership or control of these functions. Profit is not a primary goal.

The basic difference in trading with nonmarket, or socialist, countries as opposed to capitalist nations is the idea of state trading. That is, world trade is conducted through the instrumentality of the state rather than by private traders. In these economies, there is a near total monopoly of all trading institutions by the state. The government is either the principal in each transaction or it delegates that responsibility to an institution. In most nonmarket countries, this institution is usually a foreign trade corporation.

In addition to the fact that these institutions are less independent than businesses in capitalistic countries, the market forces that operate in a free market economy are absent in a nonmarket economy. For example, all other interests are subservient to a central economic plan. Thus, the world trader must concern itself with whether the activity of a foreign trade corporation is an administrative and political activity of the government or whether the activity amounts to a commercial venture.

Legal Environments

Since no single international commercial legal system exists, the legal environment for international business consists primarily of the laws and courts of the many nations of the world. These national systems vary in philosophy and practice, and each nation maintains a court system that is independent of those in every other nation.

3

Most countries derive their legal systems from the common law, the civil law, or Muslim law. **Common law** is a tradition-oriented system. The interpretation of what the law means on a given subject is influenced by previous court decisions as well as by custom and usage. If there is no specific precedent or statute, common law requires a court to make a decision that, in effect, will create new law. Common law is English in origin and is found in the United States and in the twenty-six countries that have come under English influence.

Civil law is based on a comprehensive set of laws organized into a code. Rather than relying on precedent or court interpretation, the code is intended to spell out the law in all possible situations. This need to be all-inclusive may lead to some rather general provisions, allowing an application to many types of facts and circumstances. Judges in a civil-law system resolve disputes, therefore, by direct reference to the statute in question, giving little, if any, consideration to prior court decisions. Code law is predominant in Europe and in those nations that have not had ties with England. There are about seventy civil-law countries — such as Germany, France, Japan, and the USSR — where statutes or codes are the main source of law.

Muslim law represents a third major legal system. About twenty-seven countries follow Muslim law to varying degrees, and the system is usually mixed with civil, common, and/or indigenous law, depending on previous colonial ties. In an Islamic nation where it is the dominant legal system, as in Saudi Arabia, Muslim law governs all aspects of life, for it is but one facet of the Islamic religion itself. This religion states exactly what a Muslim must believe, and it includes the *Shari'a*, which specifies how the Muslim should conduct himself, the sanction for transgressions being the state of sin. Muslim law has few civil, as opposed to spiritual, sanctions. Rules not contained in the historical sources of the *Shari'a* are made by government regulations and Islamic judges.

Organizing a Worldwide Business

A domestic company thinks multinational when its management begins to plan and organize in worldwide terms for maximizing its resources. Such a policy requires different strategies from those used in a similar domestic situation to meet the myriad economic, legal, social, political, and cultural barriers that are common in foreign legal environments.

All sovereign states impose some limitations on how foreigners may enter into their business environments. In the United States, for example, radio and television broadcasting licenses can be held only by American individuals or corporations, while France does not allow foreign ownership in their hydroelectric industry.

When considering the legal form of business organization to select, a company must realize that there are distinctions between the common law and civil law in the area of the corporate form of business. Under common law, a charter from the state gives existence to a corporation, whereas under civil law, a corporation is created by contract. In Germany, there are two forms of corporation: the GMBH is set up for the smaller enterprise, while the AG is structured for a large number of shareholders and is a public corporation. The usual methods for entering a foreign market are: (1) by means of a licensing arrangement; (2) by joint venture; or (3) by establishing a minority, majority, or wholly owned subsidiary. Whatever the final decision as to form, there will be legal implications for the amount of control that is exercised by the parent.

Finally, although the multinational enterprise will transact its business across international borders, it is a creature of domestic legal systems, not international. When it is not a single entity but rather a system of business organizations tied together by diverse legal arrangements, these organizations will be under the laws of the different nations in which they are formed.

INTERNATIONAL LAW

A simple answer to the question of what international law is is that international law is the law that governs relationships between sovereign countries, which are the basic units in the world political system. It is the public law of nations. Chief Justice Marshall offered a definition of international law in *Thirty Hogsheads of Sugar* v. *Boyle*, 9 Cranch 191, 197 (1815):

> The law of nations is the great source from which we derive those rules, . . . which are recognized by all civilized and commercial states throughout Europe and America. This law is in part unwritten, and in part conventional. To ascertain that which is unwritten, we resort to the great principles of reason and justice; but, as these principles will be differently understood by different nations under different circumstances, we consider them as being, in some degree, fixed and rendered stable by a series of judicial decisions. The decisions of the courts of

every country, so far as they are founded upon a law common to every country, will be received, not as authority, but with respect. The decisions of the courts of every country show how the law of nations in the given case is understood in that country, and will be considered in adopting the rule which is to prevail in this.

A study of international law reveals how states react, and may be expected to react, to conditions that confront them. There are rules that countries will habitually ignore because the official state position may not have kept pace with changes in world society. Likewise, there are rules that several countries may have accepted as the law for governing their mutual relations. How can there be a public law governing sovereign countries? There is no world legislature to enact such law, executive power to enforce it, or judiciary to resolve disputes over its application. Therefore, one thing is certain: compliance by a sovereign country with whatever international rules there are must be voluntary and will yield to the interest of that country in a given situation.

International law is actually becoming more than a system governing the relationships between states. As the states establish regional and supranational organizations, our understanding of what international law is changes because new rules have and will evolve to fit new situations. The practices of countries with regard to their treatment of rules of international law do not lend themselves to any logical arrangement.

Private Versus Public Law

In an expanding world market, the courts cannot possibly anticipate the "risks" of the many transactions into which traders enter. Societies, therefore, give the parties freedom of contract to allow them to accommodate their needs to those of the world community and, in effect, to negotiate a "private" law to cover a particular transaction. Private law is not the law of nations. A worldwide commercial transaction will involve parties from different nations who deal at "arm's length" and negotiate the rules based on the various risks that will apply to their final agreement. This agreement reflects whatever arrangement the parties make between themselves with respect to the place, time, and performance of their agreement, including the payment of the purchase price. In addition, within public policy limitations, the parties are able to select a domestic law to govern the transaction as well as a domestic legal system in which to resolve any disputes that might arise. Party autonomy and the security of contractual obligations are of primary importance in world commercial transactions.

The various legal systems provide for the interpretation of contracts, but the courts will not make a contract for the parties. Thus, the contract is a private affair and not a social institution.

On the other hand, world commercial transactions are some of the most regulated of activities. There are rules for exporting, importing, investing, or consulting across national borders. In addition, there are industrial, health, and safety standards, as well as packaging, labeling, and marketing regulations. This is the public law of world business. It is a form of regulation that involves legal, political, and economic factors. For example, nations may regulate world business for such reasons as solving balance of payment problems, the preservation of natural resources, the furthering of national security, and the protection of domestic industries.

Sources of International Law

The clearest source of international law are those treaties, conventions, and agreements that countries have expressly undertaken to be binding upon themselves. Evidence of what the law probably is may also be found in custom, the general principles of law recognized by civilized nations, judicial decisions, and doctrinal writings. However, the advent in this century of so many new countries made what constitutes international law a matter of controversy. Some developing countries went so far as to assert that there could be no customary law that is binding on them since they had played no part in the development of the custom. Representatives of the developing nations have also taken the position that constant reiteration of the same principle in the many resolutions that have come from various organs of the United Nations amounts to law, even though the resolutions themselves lack obligatory force. And, of course, the supernational organizations, such as the Organization of African Unity, the Organization of American States, the Council of Europe, and the European Economic Community, all make their own contributions to the body of international law.

State practice in international law as expressed in official documents and statements, indicates what a particular state perceives international law to be. When these statements are consistent over a period of time, the presumption is that that particular country is likely to consider that principle the law. When similar statements are made by a number of nations, the inference is that there is general agreement that the principle constitutes the law. Official documents and statements sometimes make reference to the decisions of international tribunals. In addition, the domestic courts of a particular country may also refer to international law. Although such references may reflect the practices of a country with regard to the laws of other nations, they are not of much use to the businessperson who wants to know a country's view on a particular aspect of international law. For example, the businessperson may find that he or she cannot enforce a contract that was made with a foreign state. In this situation, it becomes necessary not merely to find out what a particular country's attitude is toward a putative rule of international law, but also to discover how that rule is put into effect within the nation concerned.

According to English common law, public international law is part of the law of the land. This is especially true in the United States where, in accordance with the Constitution, ratified treaties will even override prior legislation. As expressed by Justice Oliver Wendell Holmes in *Missouri v. Holland*, 252 U.S. 416 (1920): "Acts of Congress are the supreme law of the land only when made in pursuance of the Constitution, while treaties are declared to be so when made under the authority of the United States. . . ."

International Business Law

What is international business law? Is it capable of definition? Where can it be found? These are some of the questions that concern business managers as they formulate international business policy.

Business laws influence what business activities may or may not take place whenever an organization imports, exports, ships, invests, or contemplates an international business activity. For example, it is necessary to consult the domestic laws in the home and the host states if a proposed activity requires the movement of people. Items such as visas, work permits, employment agreements, and employment termination clauses would be involved. On the other hand, the movement of goods raises tax, antitrust, packaging, and advertising problems. Transfers of information involve patent and trademark questions. Each international transaction raises the possibility of the extraterritorial extension of the domestic laws of the home and host states, which may result in potential conflicts. International business activity may also require consulting the trade rules of regional groups like the European Common Market. Finally, there are multilateral and bilateral treaties between the home and host states that might impinge on international business.

SUMMARY

The world trader expands across different national borders and operates in many foreign legal environments. Therefore, the world trader, unlike the wholly domestic trader, has to take into account complex and diverse legal constraints. In some cases, those constraints are not only ambiguous but may be subject to recurring change.

This overview is of necessity a general global view of the world legal environment. The next chapter will analyze the various legal relationships that are involved in world trade.

DISCUSSION QUESTIONS

1. Can there be an effective international order considering the diverse cultures, political systems, and ideologies that exist on the international scene?
2. Compare the socialistic and capitalistic systems of property ownership.
3. Why should the parties to a transaction be allowed to select a domestic law as well as a domestic legal system to govern their private transaction?
4. Can there be a law of nations in the absence of compulsory enforcement?
5. Why is international business law a creature of domestic law?

CHAPTER 2

▼

Legal Relationships Between Individuals and Nations

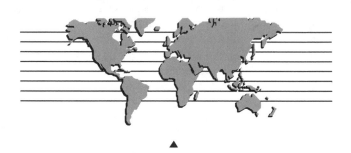

▲

It is people who engage in world trade. It is people, acting as private buyers or working through business organizations, who are responsible for the final decision to engage in trade across national borders. An understanding, therefore, of the legal relationships between individuals and nations that are created by international business transactions is necessary.

The world is made up of sovereign nations. The person who is interested in world trade needs to understand the criteria that distinguish the sovereign nation from other world organizations and the impact of sovereignty on world trade. A second dimension of the legal environment of world trade is the relationship of the individual to the sovereign nation. In their business dealings individuals form or may seek to form various links with countries. However, although a nation's laws will grant certain rights and privileges to its citizens, noncitizens or aliens may incur certain risks. People who must go abroad as part of a business transaction need to gain entry and to be permitted to work in the host nation. This chapter will examine the concept of sovereignty and the relationship of the individual to the sovereign nation as elements of the legal environment of world trade.

SOVEREIGNTY

The world is organized into a political system of sovereign nations. It is a system that has tripled in membership since the beginning of the twentieth century. In light of this rapid growth, determining which entities are entitled to membership has been essential to the operation of the system. Several criteria are considered in determining the legitimacy of a nation; some of the basic ones are

independence

an effective government

a permanent population

an economy

a defined territory

the capacity to conduct foreign relations

A primary requirement for existence as a nation is independence. An independent nation has the absolute right and power to govern its population and the various activities that occur within the confines of a specifically defined territory. These internal activities are subject only to those values and laws that are deemed permissible by that nation's government. A sovereign nation also has a separate national economy and separate national interests.

In the conduct of its relationships with other sovereign nations, a single state can accomplish as much or as little as it pleases. Its actual behavior is restrained only by its power and the power of the other sovereign nations that it deals with in the world system. Each sovereign nation seeks to promote its own national interests in its conduct of foreign relations. One of the most important of these interests is national economic growth and prosperity. Thus a state may visualize its self-interest as the encouragement of the free flow of goods, services, and people between itself and other states. Or it may be in its self-interest to regulate and suppress that flow. Quite frequently, its attitude will be the result of a clash between domestic and world interests within the state itself. For example, the communist nations are forced to make purchases in the world market whenever their five-year domestic plans fail.

Foreign relations are an exercise of sovereign power, and the relative power of nations influences their relationships. This does not mean that foreign relations will always involve conflict that is resolved by the size and power of the respective nations' armed forces. There are other more subtle forms of power, such as economic power, geographic location, political power, and the like. Neither does the exercise of power always involve an antagonistic clash of national interests. The space race is an example of the competitive and yet, in some instances, cooperative use of technological power.

Finally, to be a participant in international law, a nation must obtain recognition from the other nations in the world system. Recognition is the acknowledgment by existing nations of the nation as a legal entity and the acceptance of that entity as a member of the world system. Recognition is a political act decided upon by those government officials who are responsible for conducting foreign relations. A nation can recognize a country by a formal announcement to that effect or by entering into negotiations or by exchanging diplomats with it. Thus, recognition is a political action that is declaratory of an existing fact. It should be pointed out, however, that in principle nations may exist independent of recognition. For example, the nonrecognition of Israel by many nations does not preclude the application of international law to that country.

As a member of the world system nations (1) are presumed "equal"; (2) are sovereign, in that they are able to act independently of other nations in world affairs; (3) have exclusive rights to manage their internal affairs; and (4) are not subject, without their consent, to a compulsory jurisdiction of international law.

Business Implications of Sovereignty

Every decision maker must be aware of the implications of sovereignty and its effect on world trade. For example, each sovereign nation can pass laws governing the activities of its citizens and those of other sovereignties residing or doing business within its borders. It can impose taxes and regulations on imports, banking, investing, or any other business activity that a foreigner would like to perform within its jurisdiction. Finally, a sovereign nation may deny a business firm or individual the privilege of conducting a business within its national borders, or it may prohibit its business firms from trading with specific nations. It may also prohibit the sale of certain goods to specific countries.

THE INDIVIDUAL AND NATIONS

A fundamental principle of international law is that rights granted under international law are given to nations and, through them, to their citizens. Objections to violations of international law, therefore, must be raised by nations on behalf of their citizens. Virtually all courts recognize an exception to this principle in that nations who are parties to a treaty may grant rights to individuals who may then assert principles of international law within the limits of the treaty. It should be noted that these individual rights still belong to the state because they derive wholly from agreement between or among states and are given to individuals only by virtue of their being subjects of national law.

Traditionally, the relationship between an individual and nations is based on the common-law relationship between subject and monarch. For example, a United States citizen in England is subject to English law because the monarch has sovereignty over English territory. At the same time, the American citizen may be liable for punishment as an American citizen for what he or she did in England. Thus, an act done in one place may have legal consequences in two nations.

It is necessary to define the relationship between the individual and nations in the context of world business because the individuals who participate in world transactions are highly mobile. Owing to this fact, an individual may have links with more than one nation. These links generally consist of citizenship, nationality, domicile, and residence.

Citizenship is a relationship between an individual and a nation in which certain privileges may be granted by virtue of the individual's membership in the political community. For example, a citizen is entitled to the rights and privileges of owning land, voting, holding elective office, etc. A citizen, in turn, owes allegiance to his or her government and, at the same time, is entitled to the protection of that government. Unlike citizenship, which may be acquired or discarded, nationality is a person's natural political affiliation, acquired at birth, with all its rights, duties, and obligations. American laws refer to two ways of acquiring nationality: by place of birth *(jus suli);* and through the nationality of one or both of the parents *(jus sanguinis).*

Naturalization is an alternative route to birth for acquiring citizenship. It is based on a concept that is unknown to some legal systems, that is, an individual should be free to leave his or her country, give up his or her nationality, and acquire a new citizenship. The naturalization of an individual is an exercise by a state of its domestic jurisdiction. To

13

have international legitimacy a naturalized citizen must have a genuine connection with the new state in terms of social, economic, or religious interests.

Domicile is the relationship between an individual and the nation that can be identified as his or her home. A person who is living in a country is deemed to be a subject of that country, and he or she owes allegiance to that country while living there. Therefore, mere lawful presence in a country creates an implied assurance of safe conduct and certain rights. These rights become more extensive and secure if the person indicates an intention to become a citizen of that country, and these rights expand to those of full citizenship upon naturalization. A residence may be a temporary home or dwelling place, that is, transient in nature as on a business trip. The distinction between domicile and residence is the permanency of the former and the temporary nature of the latter.

International Migration

Two basic reasons for general international migration of persons are the desire for better employment and the search for an improved standard of living. The absence of economic opportunity in the home country is often severe enough to spur migration to developed countries even if job opportunities are nonexistent. The risks attendant upon being denied employment in a new country because of one's immigration status are not as important as the day-to-day risks of survival in some home countries.

Undocumented workers are often willing to work for wages and under working conditions that are not acceptable to their domestic counterparts. Certain sectors of the American economy — the garment industry, for example — have become highly dependent upon these workers because of increasing competition from low-wage workers in similar enterprises abroad. Other sectors of the economy, such as the restaurant industry, have turned to undocumented workers as a way of delivering low-cost products, which, of course, results in higher profits.

Immigration Policy

The formulation of an immigration policy for a nation is a task requiring the balancing of foreign and domestic policies. United States immigration policy is linked to trade policy, national security and energy policies, relations with developing countries, the domestic economy, and the civil rights of American citizens. Likewise, economic and demographic phenomena must be considered in the formulation of immigration policy. For example, the significant presence of undocumented workers of Mexican origin is affected on the United States side by our need for labor, by our need for ample and secure energy resources, and by a concern for the political stability of a neighboring country; and on the Mexican side by economic underdevelopment and the need for technology and investment capital, by the population explosion, and by treatment of Mexican nationals within the United States.

Control of Migration

In the world society the citizens of one sovereign nation are aliens in relation to every other nation. Therefore, when a nation invites aliens to cross its borders, it does so as a matter of practical politics and national self-interest. Accordingly, a nation may decide to restrict the right of immigration, totally exclude immigration, or allow it on a selective and exclusionary basis. In the case of *Nishimura Ekiu* v. *U.S.*, 142 U.S. 651, 659 (1892), the court said:

> . . . It is an accepted maxim of international law that every sovereign nation has the power, as inherent in sovereignty, and essential to self-preservation, to forbid the entrance of foreigners within its dominions, or to admit them in such cases and upon such conditions as it may see fit to prescribe. . . .

As a general rule, all countries require that foreigners possess a valid passport as a prerequisite to crossing their borders. The passport is, in effect, a letter of introduction from the issuing sovereign that vouches for the bearer and his or her conduct and requests other sovereigns to give any necessary assistance to the bearer. In some countries the possession of a passport is the only way a person can lawfully leave his or her country. The issuance of a passport is subject to reasonable government regulation, such as for reasons of national security and foreign policy considerations.

A country may also issue entry visas for varying purposes and for varying periods of time, and it may exclude certain categories of individuals from qualifying for a visa. Countries differ as to the extent to which one visa may be valid for reentry into the issuing country. In the United States, for example, the Immigration and Naturalization Act of 1952 allows for the following business visas: B-1 (visitor for business); E-1 (treaty trader); E-2 (treaty investor); and L-1 (intracompany transfer).

15

There is no prescribed limit on the total length of time a person may remain in the United States as an employee or as a self-employed person under an E-type visa. The E-type visitor comes "solely to carry on substantial trade, principally between the United States and the foreign state of which he is a national" or "to develop and direct the operations of an enterprise in which he has invested . . . a substantial amount of capital." The initial period of admission under an E-type visa may not exceed one year; an extension may be granted in periods of not more than one year.

The foreign investor who requests entry with an intention to either purchase an existing business or to begin one of his or her own is assigned a B-1 visa. The B-1 temporary visitor may not engage in gainful employment while a visitor nor may the B-1 holder receive U.S.-source income. The B-1 visa is granted for a period of one year and may be renewed for six-month periods.

The L-1 visa allows a corporation to transfer to the United States a person whom it has employed for at least one year abroad in one of its branches, subsidiaries, or affiliates. To qualify, the employee must come to the United States to serve in a managerial capacity or in a capacity that requires special knowledge or skills. Unlike the E category, the L-1 visa does not require a treaty to exist between the alien's home nation and the United States. The length of the visa is generally five years, with the possibility of extensions being granted.

Deportation

Each sovereign nation has the inherent right to deport or expel all aliens, or any class of aliens, absolutely or upon certain conditions. This right is essential to a nation's safety, its independence, and its welfare. Aliens residing in the United States, so long as they are permitted to remain, are entitled to the safeguards of the Constitution and to the protection of the laws in regard to their persons and property. They also must assume their civil and criminal responsibilities. However, as they continue to be aliens, they remain subject to the power of the nation to order them to be removed or deported from the United States whenever their removal is necessary or expedient to the public interest. It should be noted that any policy toward aliens is part of the conduct of foreign relations, the war power, and the maintenance of a democratic form of government. For this reason, the judiciary is sometimes reluctant to deal with matters concerning aliens because policies concerning them are essentially political in nature.

SUMMARY

The movement of people is a primary factor to be considered in making decisions about world trade. The world trader must understand the various relationships that exist between individuals and sovereign nations. That it is a sovereign right for a nation to control international migration of people in its own self-interest is fundamental. Immigration policy determines whether or not a business firm may send people into other nations, for how long a period of time, and whether or not they will be expelled.

In the next chapter the various international agreements that control the conduct of business between nations will be analyzed.

SUGGESTED CASE READINGS

The Schooner Exchange v. *McFaddon*, 7 Cranch 116 (1812).

Blackmer v. *U.S.*, 284 U.S. 421 (1922).

In Re Estate of Jones, 182 N.W. 227 (1921).

"*S.S. Lotus*", (1927) P.C.I.J., sec. A., No. 10.

Republic of Vietnam v. *Pfizer, Inc.*, 556 F.2d 892 (1977).

DISCUSSION QUESTIONS

1. What are the criteria to consider in determining the legitimacy of a nation in the world system?
2. What are the legal presumptions with regard to membership in the world system?
3. Discuss the business implications of sovereignty.
4. Explain the various relationships that exist between an individual and nations.
5. What is the source of a nation's power to exclude aliens? To conditionally admit them? To expel or deport them?

CHAPTER 3

▼

International Agreements

▲

Although the world system is made up of sovereign nations that are "equal," international law does not presume that these nations have economic equality. It remains true, however, that one of the attributes of sovereignty is that each nation has control over its economy. Therefore, it is up to each nation to decide for itself whether, and in what form, it will grant equal treatment in matters of world trade to other nations, or if it will give privileged treatment to some nations and discriminate against others.

The primary method by which world governments cooperate with other world governments in matters of trade is through international agreements. If a government is to attain the goals of its economic policy, it must have both an efficient and flexible procedure for entering into agreements with other world governments. These agreements are sometimes referred to as *pacts, protocols, conventions, charters,* and an *exchange of notes and concordats,* in addition to *treaties.* In the United States, for example, the executive must not only be able to act promptly in the treaty-making process but, at the same time, have an understanding that it will be supported by the other branches of the government. Likewise, other governments must know, if they are willing to undertake joint commitments, that the United States can implement such agreements.

Article II, section 2, of the U.S. Constitution gives the President the power "by and with the Advice and Consent of the Senate, to make Treaties." In addition, the Constitution gives to the President and to the Congress broad powers of control over external relations of the government. In order to implement these powers, the President and the Congress have the authority to make intergovernmental agreements and to give these agreements legal standing.

TREATIES

A treaty is an agreement that binds only the parties to it. When there are two parties, it is a *bilateral* treaty; in situations where there are more than two nations involved, the agreement is a *multilateral* treaty. A nation becomes a party by "ratifying," "approving," "accepting," "acceding," or "adhering" to a treaty under the authority granted to its executive for accomplishing that task.

Treaties determine the rules under which world traders can export to, or conduct business activities within, each other's territory. Tariff accords, income tax conventions, and treaties of friendship, commerce, and navigation purport to regulate trade problems that impede or distort trade by defining the rights and obligations of the parties or by providing for the enforcement of judgments in the case of disputes. Thus, the treaty is a means of bringing some predictability, uniformity, and order to world trade.

The term *treaty* was defined in the Vienna Convention on the Law of Treaties of 1969 as any of those "international agreements concluded between States in written form and governed by international law," which are "binding upon the parties" to them and "must be performed by them in good faith." There are other "international agreements" that nations or persons acting on behalf of nations have subscribed to, without regard to their being binding, or enforceable, or subject to an obligation of performance in good faith. These agreements would include executive agreements, declarations of policy, joint communiques or resolutions of the United Nations General Assembly, and other commitments of varying types made by various levels of government.

Treaties whereby nations enter into alliances, or agree to coordinate military action, or lay out their agreed policies for the future are deemed *political treaties*. There is a practical awareness that these agreements cannot be enforced. For example, if a nation refuses to come to the aid of another under the terms of an alliance, nothing can force it to. Similarly, if a nation changes its policy and leaves an alliance, only political or economic pressure can bring about a reversal of that position.

Treaties sometimes contain a provision calling for negotiations to conclude further, more detailed agreements. The Treaty of Rome of 1957 establishing the European Economic Community contains a number of such provisions. The Montevideo Treaty of 1960 instituting a Latin American Free Trade Area calls for negotiations among the contracting parties with a view to drawing up schedules for the reduction or elimination of customs duties and other trade restrictions.

In the United States, international agreements involve complicated problems of federalism and of the interrelationships between the executive power to manage foreign relations and the power of the legislature. The relationship of treaties to conflicting laws and to the allocation of power between the state and the federal government and their effect on business agreements have been the subject of numerous court decisions. In *Foster* v. *Neilson*, 2 Pet. 253, 314 (1829), Chief Justice Marshall discussed the concept of a treaty:

> A treaty is in its nature a contract between two nations, not a Legislative Act. It does not generally effect, of itself, the object to be accomplished, especially so far as its operation is intraterritorial; but is carried into execution by the sovereign power of the respective parties to the instrument.
>
> In the United States a different principle is established. Our Constitution declares a treaty to be the law of the land. It is, consequently, to be regarded in courts of justice as equivalent to an Act of the Legislature, whenever it operates of itself without the aid of any legislative provision. But when the terms import a contract — when either of the parties engages to perform a particular act — the treaty addresses itself to the political, not the judicial department; and the Legislature must execute the contract before it can become a rule for the court.

Marshall distinguished between treaties that are "self-executing" and those that are "non-self-executing." A treaty that requires no legislation to make it operative is said to be "self-executing." There is also a general requirement that treaties not conflict with the Constitution in order to have "binding force and effect" within the United States.

In international law the principle that applies to treaties is that "treaties ought to be observed." The notion of a binding treaty was discussed by Justice Millet in the *Head Money Cases*, 112 U.S. 580, 598–599 (1884).

> A treaty is primarily a compact between independent nations. It depends for the enforcement of its provisions on the interest and the honor of the governments which are parties to it. If these fail, its infraction becomes the subject of international negotiations and reclamations, so far as the injured party chooses to seek redress, which may in the end be enforced by actual wars. It is obvious that with this the judicial courts have nothing to do and can give no redress. But a treaty may also contain provisions which confer certain rights upon the citizens or subjects of one of the nations residing in the territorial limits of the other, which partake of the nature of municipal law, and which are capable of enforcement as between private parties in the courts of the country. . . .
>
> A treaty, then, is a law of the land as an act of Congress is, whenever its provisions prescribe a rule by which the rights of the private citizen or subject may be determined. And when such rights are of a nature to be enforced in a court of justice, that court resorts to the treaty for a rule of decision for the case before as it would to a statute. . . .

However, if the parties believe that the continuation of a treaty is contrary to their own national interests, the agreement can be terminated by the consent of the parties to the agreement.

Rules of Interpretation

The general rules for the interpretation of treaties as developed by the courts are as follows:

1. All treaty provisions should be given sensible meanings, if that is practicable.
2. A treaty is to be read in the light of the conditions and circumstances existing at the time it was entered into, with a view to effecting the objects and purposes of the contracting parties.
3. The language of the treaty, however, is not to be given a strained construction or an unreasonable interpretation in order to vouchsafe to aliens rights and privileges denied to citizens.
4. Treaties are to be liberally construed so as to effect the apparent intention of the parties.

5. When a treaty provision fairly admits of two constructions, one restricting, the other enlarging rights that may be claimed under it, the more liberal interpretation is to be preferred.

6. The meaning of treaty provisions is not restricted by any necessity of avoiding possible conflict with state legislation and must prevail over inconsistent state enactments.

7. When the meaning of treaty provisions is uncertain, recourse may be had to the negotiations and diplomatic correspondence of the contracting parties relating to the subject matter and to their own practical construction of it.

Terminating Treaties

As a rule, either contracting party may terminate a treaty upon the giving of formal notice. A treaty is likewise terminated if the parties enter into a new treaty that by implication supersedes the first pact. In those situations when one signing party publicly renounces a treaty, mutual consent is inferred if the other party fails to protest or acts in a manner inconsistent with the treaty. Finally, a treaty is considered terminated once its purpose is fulfilled.

Treaties of Friendship, Commerce, and Navigation

The United States negotiates many bilateral treaties for the protection and encouragement of U.S. trade and investment overseas. The "treaty of friendship, commerce, and navigation" is a familiar title in American foreign relations. It should be noted that, although the term *friendship* appears in the title and this presupposes friendliness and goodwill between the parties, these treaties are not viewed as being primarily political in character. They are simply economic and legal agreements designed to further a nation's self-interest.

The treaty of friendship, commerce, and navigation covers a wide range of factors that the basic agreement must address:

entry of individuals

entry of goods

entry of ships and cargoes

entry of capital

acquisition of property

protection of persons and property

transfer of funds

The basic objective of these agreements is to obligate each contracting country to ensure reciprocal respect for each other's national interests according to agreed rules of law. As such, they attempt to define the treatment each nation owes the citizens of the other: their rights with respect to doing business and other activities within the boundaries of the host nation. It spells out the respect due them, their property, and their business enterprises.

Generally, the scope of commercial treaties is such that, to be both durable and workable, their operative rules must be stated in simple terms. In this area there are two contingent standards that traditionally define the kind of treatment provided. Initially, the "most-favored-nation" clause was used at a time when discrimination in commercial dealing was the general rule between nations. It meant that one contracting nation would make concessions only when the other nation made concessions. In other words, the policy was conditional, and most-favored-nation treatment meant the privilege to bargain for such treatment. The economically more powerful nations did, however, follow an unconditional most-favored-nation policy. For example, each concession the United States made to another country was extended to all nations to whom we were obligated by treaty to give most-favored-nation treatment. Today, first-class treatment is "national" treatment, which implies that the foreign citizen and the foreign citizen's property will be treated in substantially the same manner as that of the citizens of the country granting "national" treatment. The policy is an attempt to impose a principle of nondiscrimination like that which applies to goods that are domestically produced and goods that are imported.

The exchange of most-favored-nation treatment between non-market-economy and market-economy nations generally favors the nonmarket state. This is true because the government of a nonmarket nation collects tariffs (from itself) and purchases all imports. Therefore, the lower tariffs that are generated by most-favored-nation treatment produce no greater incentive to import because the level of tariffs does not affect the price that the government pays for imports. However, in a market-economy nation, lower tariffs enhance the attractiveness of imports by lowering the price that the private buyer must pay for them. As a result, market-economy states usually seek further concessions from nonmarket nations.

Taxation Treaties

By engaging in world trade, business firms and individuals may come under the jurisdiction of more than one taxing authority. Therefore, the questions arise: how is the firm/individual to be taxed and how can it avoid paying taxes on the same base to more than one of the taxing jurisdictions?

The right to levy and collect taxes is a basic right of the sovereign, but the tax systems of the different nations vary considerably. For example, there is disagreement over who is to be taxed, the concepts of residency of the business and the individual, and what is income. The United States has bilateral taxation treaties with many nations, all of which are intended to provide relief from double taxation.

The growth of world trade has led to increased evasion of foreign tax liability. This trend is likely to intensify as economic interdependence of nations increases and taxpayers become aware of their ability to legally evade a foreign tax liability by crossing national boundaries. As a general rule, U.S. tax treaties contain collection provisions intended to prevent such evasion. Under the terms of these agreements, the parties express a willingness to aid in the collection of all taxes covered by the treaty. The general collection provision in a typical tax treaty states:

> The Contracting States undertake to lend assistance and support to each other in the collection of taxes which are the subject of the present Convention, together with interest costs, in addition to the taxes and fines not being of a penal character.

In application, however, general collection provisions are limited. For example, they are ineffective in preventing the method of international tax evasion whereby a taxpayer flees a foreign nation and returns to his or her country of citizenship without paying a foreign tax liability. They do, however, eliminate a taxpayer's ability to evade domestic tax liability by fleeing his or her home country to a nation that has such a treaty with the United States.

THE TREATY-MAKING PROCESS IN THE UNITED STATES

The making of a treaty generally begins with face-to-face negotiations conducted by the President or his representatives with authorized representatives of the foreign nation or nations. These negotiations will, it is hoped, result in an agreement, although there may be, in addition, an international requirement that a national legislative body approve the treaty before it becomes effective. In the United States, the President is required by the Constitution to submit the treaty to the Senate for "advice and consent." Although the Constitution is silent on the details of ratification, the U.S. Senate since 1979 has claimed the right to amend and modify treaties once they have been submitted for consideration. The Supreme Court stated in *Haver* v. *Yaker*, 9 Wall. 32, 35 (1869):

> In this country, a treaty is something more than a contract, for the Federal Constitution declares it to be the law of the land. If so, before it can become a law, the Senate, in whom rests the authority to ratify it, must agree to it. . . .

Any of the Senate's reservations must be included by the President in any final act of ratification. The treaty is then put before the Senate and must receive a required two-thirds vote of those present. If this should happen, the President may ratify the treaty, although he is not bound to do so.

Finally, there is an exchange of signed instruments between the parties of a multilateral treaty, and the instrument may be deposited with a designated international organization. The President at that time will proclaim the treaty as a matter of public record, or the treaty document may state when it becomes effective.

Executive Agreements

What may be properly accomplished by treaty may also be accomplished by executive agreement. Executive agreements are not mentioned in the Constitution, in the Constitutional Convention, or in the Ratification Conventions, so they are considered to be part of the President's independent powers. And although they cover foreign relations, an executive agreement is entered into without the advice and consent of the Senate. In fact, the Supreme Court has held that the powers of the President in the conduct of foreign policy need not be restricted by the need for "advice and consent."

Executive agreements fall into two categories: (1) those authorized by Congress; and (2) those made solely on presidential authority and negotiated personally by the executive branch in a wide range of areas. For example, early in our history, Congress authorized the President to borrow money from other countries. Texas became a U.S. possession through an executive agreement approved by a resolution of Congress. The President is also able to lower tariff barriers in general and reduce restrictions on international trade by executive agreement. In effect, these agreements have the same status as treaties under international law and the domestic law of the United States.

Presidents have generally shown a preference for executive agreements because they provide greater flexibility in negotiations and more control over the outcome. Additionally, the use of executive agreement avoids the debate and delay of the treaty-ratification process. The executive agreement may come into effect on the date of signature if it needs no further legislative action. By an increasing use of executive agreements, the President has significantly increased his power in foreign affairs. For example, on January 1, 1972, there were in force a total of 947 treaties and 4,359 executive agreements. Executive agreements now outnumber treaties four to one and are used more and more frequently.

The Transmittal Act of 1972

The Congress has expressed concern that it is not being adequately informed about the content and growing number of executive agreements. One step taken in formally recognizing congressional concern in this area was the passage of the Transmittal Act of 1972. The Act reads as follows:

> The Secretary of State shall transmit to the Congress the text of any international agreement, other than a treaty, to which the United States is a party as soon as practicable after such agreement has entered into force with respect to the United States but in no event later than sixty days thereafter. However, any such agreement the immediately public disclosure of which would, in the opinion of the President, be prejudicial to the national security of the United States shall not be transmitted to the Congress but shall be transmitted to the committee on Foreign Affairs of the House of Representatives un-

der an appropriate injunction of secrecy to be removed only upon due notice from the President. 1 U.S.C. §112B (1972)

The Transmittal Act does not fully resolve the problem of executive secrecy in foreign policy issues. If the President decides to keep an agreement secret and refuses to divulge its existence to the Congress, the Act has no provision for compelling the executive to do otherwise.

Presidential Authorizations

The President has been broadly "authorized" to suspend embargo acts passed by Congress, "if in his judgment the public interest should require it" or if, "in the judgment of the President," there has been such suspension of hostilities abroad as may render commerce of the United States sufficiently safe.

Likewise, Congress has passed numerous acts laying tonnage and other duties on foreign ships in retaliation for duties enforced on U.S. vessels, but providing that if such duties were repealed or abolished, then the President might by proclamation suspend the duties on vessels of the nation so acting. Thus, the President has been "authorized" to proclaim the suspension; or if the President "shall be satisfied" that the discriminating duties have been abolished, the suspension will take effect; or the President "may direct" that the tonnage duty shall cease to be levied in such circumstances.

SUMMARY

International agreements, specifically treaties, represent an effective means of introducing some stability and uniformity into world trade. In the myriad of bilateral treaties entered into by the United States, the most important is the friendship, commerce, and navigation treaty. There are also treaties for the avoidance of multiple taxation, treaties dealing with tariffs, and treaties dealing with specific property groups. These agreements have a direct impact upon those individuals who engage in world trade since they constitute the rules that govern the movement of goods, persons, and money across international borders. Since these agreements regulate business activities in each of the contracting parties' territories, world traders can trade with a reasonable assurance of predictability in their transactions if nations abide by the treaties. Treaties are the public law of world trade.

The legal aspects of the multinational enterprise will be discussed at length in the next chapter.

SUGGESTED CASE READINGS

Foster v. *Neilson*, 2 Pet. 253 (1829).

The Head Money Cases, 112 U.S. 580 (1884).

U.S. v. *Vetco Inc.*, 644 F.2d 1324 (1981).

Tag v. *Rogers*, 267 F.2d 664 (1959).

State of Missouri v. *Holland*, 252 U.S. 416 (1920).

U.S. v. *Guy Capps, Inc.*, 204 F.2d 644 (1953).

DISCUSSION QUESTIONS

1. Distinguish between a self-executing and a nonself-executing treaty.
2. How do international agreements introduce stability into world trade?
3. Discuss the concepts of conditional and unconditional most-favored-nation treatment.
4. What is the basic objective of concluding a treaty of friendship, commerce, and navigation?
5. What are the various types of international agreements? How are they used to regulate world trade?

CHAPTER 4

▼

The Multinational Enterprise

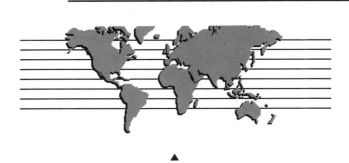

▲

The multinational enterprise begins its existence as a well-established domestic corporation that is attempting to optimize both the source and the allocation of its resources by seeking outlets in world markets. It is both a national enterprise and a business whose operations are carried on outside its country's borders. The goals of the multinational are initially economic. Depending, however, on its size, economic goals may eventually become political ones because of national policy changes in the home and host countries.

The term *multinational enterprise* is synonymous with *multinational corporation*. Either is commonly used today in the literature of international business. The term *transnational corporation* is also sometimes used interchangeably with *multinational enterprise,* but throughout this text, the term employed will be *multinational enterprise.*

The business activities of the enterprise involve either private or governmental relationships. In the case of the private firm, business activities are purely profit motivated, whereas the governmental trader may or may not be primarily profit oriented. In either case, the international business activities of the multinational include the buying and selling of goods; investing in local industry; the licensing of technology; and the supplying of personal services, such as legal, marketing, and management consulting.

A multinational enterprise is not always a single legal entity because it may conduct its business activities in a number of different ways. It may, then, be defined as an economic system that has supply, production, and marketing units in different foreign countries. Generally, this system may be tied together by stock ownership or contractual arrangements. For example, a wholly owned subsidiary may be in one country, a parent branch in another, a joint venture in a third, and a licensing agreement in a fourth. The final choice as to the form of business depends on a number of factors. In terms of capital, the decision might be based on the amount the firm decides to commit in a host country. If the goal is to manufacture a specific product, costs of shipping and production will influence the decision. The operating rules for multinationals set down by the host country are also a determining factor. Whatever the decision, management must be able to control the various entities and legal arrangements within its power structure to have an effective business operation.

In recent years, the expanded worldwide role of multinational enterprises has attracted considerable attention. Their economic and, in some cases, political power has created difficulties for both the home and host countries that seek to exercise legal authority over them. The multinational enterprise system has a primary impact in shaping trade, investment, and technology transfers worldwide, and its activities have direct bearing on the balance of payments, production, trade, employment, growth, and the international competitive climate of individual countries. National governments seek to regulate and control multinationals according to their individual perceived national interests, but are frustrated by the ability of these firms to escape national jurisdiction in matters of taxation, market monopolation, and other business policy areas. In these situations, the multinational is considered a private enterprise and, as such, is subject to applicable domestic law in the host country. Hence, like an individual, the multinational system must rely on the protection of its home government, since it does not have access to international legal tribunals to protect itself.

ENTERING A HOST COUNTRY

The original decision to become multinational is made in an attempt to increase profits by expanding the firm's market for its products to a particular foreign market. This decision takes into consideration such factors as market potential, raw materials, the labor force, capital, government incentives, taxes, exchange controls, local participation, and political and economic stability. Note that from both a legal and an economic viewpoint all of these factors are subject to change. Generally, entry into the host country is accomplished by means of a legal arrangement that offers such advantages as

> facilitating local participation and local financing
>
> minimizing the publicizing of business activities outside the host country
>
> eliminating confusion as to local legal status
>
> maximizing tax benefits between home and host countries

The decision takes into consideration the laws and regulations that govern entry into the host country. Approval of a government agency may be required or specific approval for entry in certain areas, or there may be an outright ban on foreign investment in certain sensitive industries. A final consideration is the nature of the treaties between the home and host nations (see Chapter 3).

Historically, the argument was that in the interpretation of the treaties such words as *citizen*, *national*, or *subject* applied to corporations as well as to individuals. Strictly speaking, however, these terms imply relationships that are personal in nature and that can only be possessed by an individual. Therefore, in international business law, corporations must be expressly mentioned to be included within the provisions of a treaty, as in Article VIII, paragraph 1, in the Japan Treaty of 1953: "Nationals and companies of either Party shall be accorded national treatment with respect to engaging in all types of commercial, industrial, financial and other business activities. . . ."

Foreign Investment Codes

As an incentive to encourage foreign investment, many nations have adopted foreign investment codes. These laws are designed to minimize some of the uncertainties of a foreign venture for an investor. Typically, the foreign investment code provides for the negotiation of investment agreements between the foreign investor and the host government, covering such items as taxes, transfers of monies, and the guarantee of prompt and adequate payment in the event of an expropriation. A policy of selective promotion in the code attempts to channel foreign investment into those activities that contribute to the economic development of the host nation — scientific and technological development, for example, or the development of export markets.

Concession Agreements

A concession agreement or, more recently, a development agreement is a method by which the multinational is able to assure itself of a political climate conducive to foreign investment. In fact, in some countries there can be no foreign investment without a formal concession agreement with the host government. Oftentimes, foreign investment codes, which cover virtually all types of investments, serve the same purpose as concession agreements.

A concession agreement is a detailed arrangement granting a foreign investor the right to engage in stated activities in the host country. At the same time, it imposes on the investor a series of related rights and obligations. Although it is contractual in nature, the concession agreement is not a typical contractual arrangement. One of the concession agreement's distinctive characteristics is that the government of the host country is not only a contracting party but also a lawmaker who enacts the laws pertaining to concession agreements. Therefore, the host country may make its own rules for interpretation and any possible remedies available to the other contracting parties. At the same time, the government is also a sovereign that will act in its own best interests. Concession agreements vary among countries and industries. As a rule, the concession agreement involves the exploitation of a natural resource or the construction and management of a public utility. However, a number of manufacturing arrangements have also been negotiated.

At the outset of the negotiations for a concession agreement, the host country generally lacks the skills, technological know-how, capital, or even actual knowledge of the extent of its natural resources. Therefore, the multinational is given the exclusive rights to extract the natural resource in a stated area. At the same time, it is usually given the responsibility of building housing and other production facilities and is required to employ and train local personnel. Arrangements with respect to the setting of prices, exporting to third-country markets, and sharing of profits with the host government are also included. The result is that the host country is somewhat dependent upon the capital and skills of its foreign partner.

Since these arrangements have an impact on the total economic development of the host country, in time they are apt to generate disputes. For example, as the profits grow, demands may arise that the multinational contribute more capital toward the development of the host's economy. Later, the government may demand a greater responsibility for local personnel, or it may demand a larger share of the enterprise for local shareholders. It may demand a greater share of the profits, which may take the form of taxes, or change exchange control regulations, or, as a final solution, it may take over the venture (see Chapter 5).

THE LEGAL STATUS OF THE MULTINATIONAL

Treaties

Some of the more important changes in postwar trading are the worldwide use of the corporate form of organization and its inclusion in treaties. Businesspersons deal with corporations and other associations to the same degree that they deal with individuals. Such matters as the right to do business, taxation on a nondiscriminatory basis, the ability to purchase and enjoy real and personal property, and the equitable application of exchange controls are presently considered corporate as well as individual rights. Likewise, corporations as well as individuals now have substantial rights in connection with forming local subsidiaries under the corporation laws of many countries and controlling and managing the affairs of these local companies.

The inclusion of corporate rights in treaties likewise underwent a slow evolution. Treaties were initially used solely to promote trade and to protect instruments of trade; they were not concerned with the rights of traders. In pre-World War II treaties, corporations were not commonly recognized as organizations engaging in international business. Consider the following provision in a 1911 treaty with Japan:

> Limited liability and other companies and associations . . . already or hereafter to be organized in accordance with the laws of either High Contracting Party and domiciled in the territories of such party, are authorized, in the territories of the other, to exercise their rights and appear in the courts either as plaintiffs or defendants, subject to the laws of such other party.

> The foregoing stipulation has no bearing upon the question whether a company or association organized in one of the two coun-

tries will or will not be permitted to transact its business or industry in the other, this permission remaining always subject to the laws and regulations enacted or established in the respective countries or in any part thereof.

Corporate Nationality

Nationality is determined by the domestic law of each country. For a relationship of nationality to exist, there must be a genuine connection between a country and the alleged claimant to nationality. The United States invokes this concept of genuine connection. It is traditional, therefore, to attribute to a corporation the nationality either of the country in which it is incorporated or of the country in which it has its registered office. In addition, the corporation may also be considered a national of the country from which it is managed.

The question arises as to what protection a nation can offer its multinational enterprises. The following excerpts from the *Barcelona Traction* case [Case Concerning The Barcelona Traction, Light and Power Company, Limited *(Belgium v. Spain)*, Second Phase, International Court of Justice (1970) I.C. J. 3] suggest that increased attention should be given to the domicile of the shareholder of the multinational firm.

> . . . The claim is presented on behalf of natural and juristic persons, alleged to be Belgian nationals and shareholders in the Barcelona Traction, Light and Power Company, Limited. The submissions of the Belgian Government make it clear that the object of its Application is reparation for damage allegedly caused to these persons by the conduct, said to be contrary to international law, of various organs of the Spanish State towards that company and various other companies in the same group.
>
> . . . The States which the present case principally concerns are Belgium, the national State of the alleged shareholders, Spain, the State whose organs are alleged to have committed the unlawful acts complained of, and Canada, the State under whose laws Barcelona Traction was incorporated and in whose territory it has its registered office. . . .
>
> . . . When a State admits into its territory foreign investments or foreign nationals, whether natural or juristic persons, it is bound to extend to them the protection of the law and assumes obligations concerning the treatment to be afforded them. . . .
>
> . . . In seeking to determine the law applicable . . . , the Court has to bear in mind the continuous evolution of international law . . .

From its origins closely linked with international commerce, diplomatic protection has sustained a particular impact from the growth of international economic relations. . . .

. . . In allocating corporate entities to States for purposes of diplomatic protection, international law is based, but only to a limited extent, on an analogy with the rules governing the nationality of individuals. The traditional rule attributes the right of diplomatic protection of a corporate entity to the State under the laws of which it is incorporated and in whose territory it has its registered office. These two criteria have been confirmed by long practice and by numerous international instruments. This notwithstanding, further or different links are at times said to be required in order that a right of diplomatic protection should exist. Indeed, it has been the practice of some States to give a company incorporated under their law diplomatic protection solely when it has its seat . . . or management or center of control in their territory, or when a majority or a substantial proportion of the shares has been owned by nationals of the State concerned. Only then, it has been held, does there exist between the corporation and the State in question a genuine connection of the kind familiar from other branches of international law. However, in the particular field of the diplomatic protection of corporate entities, no absolute test of the "genuine connection" has found general acceptance. Such tests as have been applied are of a relative nature, and sometimes links with one State have had to be weighed against those with another. . . .

. . . In the present case . . . the company was incorporated in Canada and has its registered office in that country. . . . Not only did the founders of the company seek its incorporation under Canadian law but it has remained under that law for a period of over fifty years. It has maintained in Canada its registered office, its accounts and its share registers. Board meetings were held there for many years; it has been listed in the records of the Canadian tax authorities. Thus a close and permanent connection has been established, fortified by the passage of over half a century. This connection is in no way weakened by the fact that the company engaged from the very outset in commercial activities outside Canada, for that was its declared object. . . .

. . . The Court considers that the adoption of the theory of diplomatic protection of shareholders as such, by opening the door to competing diplomatic claims, could create an atmosphere of confusion and insecurity in international economic relations. The danger would be all the greater inasmuch as the shares of companies whose activities are international are widely scattered and frequently change hands. It might perhaps be claimed that, if the right of protection belonging to the national States of the shareholders were considered as only secondary to that of the national State of the company, there would be less danger of difficulties of the kind contemplated. . . .

. . . The situations in which foreign shareholders in a company wish to have recourse to diplomatic protection by their own national State may vary. It may happen that the national State of the company simply refuses to grant it its diplomatic protection, or that it begins to exercise it . . . but does not pursue its action to the end. It may also happen that the national State of the company and the State which has committed a violation of international law with regard to the company arrive at a settlement of the matter, by agreeing on compensation for the company, but that the foreign shareholders find the compensation insufficient. Now, as a matter of principle, it would be difficult to draw a distinction between these three cases so far as the protection of foreign shareholders by their national State is concerned, since in each case they may have suffered real damage. Furthermore, the national State of the company is perfectly free to decide how far it is appropriate for it to protect the company, and is not bound to make public the reasons for its decision. To reconcile this discretionary power of the company's national State with a right of protection falling to the shareholders' national State would be particularly difficult when the former State has concluded, with the State which has contravened international law with regard to the company, an agreement granting the company compensation which the foreign shareholders find inadequate. If, after such a settlement, the national State of the foreign shareholders could in its turn put forward a claim based on the same facts, this would be likely to introduce into the negotiation of this kind of agreement a lack of security which would be contrary to the stability which it is the object of international law to establish in international relations.

. . . It is quite true . . . that international law recognizes parallel rights of protection in the case of a person in the service of an international organization. Nor is the possibility excluded of concurrent claims being made on behalf of persons having dual nationality, although in that case lack of a genuine link with one of the two States may be set up against the exercise by that State of the right of protection. It must be observed, however, that in these two types of situations the number of possible protectors is necessarily very small, and their identity normally not difficult to determine. In this respect such cases of dual protection are markedly different from the claims to which recognition of a general right of protection of foreign shareholders by their various national States might give rise.

. . . It should also be observed that the promoters of a company whose operations will be international must take into account the fact that States have, with regard to their nationals, a discretionary power to grant diplomatic protection or to refuse it. When establishing a company in a foreign country, its promoters are normally impelled by particular considerations; it is often a question of tax or other advantages offered by the host State. It does not seem to be in any way inequitable that the advantages thus obtained should be balanced by the risks arising from the fact that the protection of the company and hence of its shareholders is thus entrusted to a State other than the national State of the shareholders.

. . . It is clear from what has been said above that Barcelona Traction was never reduced to a position of impotence such that it could not have approached its national State, Canada, to ask for its diplomatic protection, and that, as far as appeared to the Court, there was nothing to prevent Canada from continuing to grant its diplomatic protection to Barcelona Traction if it had considered that it should do so.

. . . For the above reasons, the Court is not of the opinion that, in the particular circumstances of the present case, *jus standi* [standing to sue] is conferred on the Belgian Government by considerations of equity.

. . . Accordingly,

The Court

rejects the Belgian Government's claim by fifteen votes to one, twelve votes of the majority being based on the reasons set out in the present Judgment.

THE MULTINATIONAL AND POLITICS

Social Awareness

The multinational enterprise is seen as an agent of change by the host country. However, it is also viewed as an agent of control and manipulation. Initially, the multinational is used by the host nation to effect social and economic change for desired economic prosperity. Therefore, the multinational must recognize its host's long-range development policy and plans and adjust its own goals accordingly. This means that the multinational has to adapt its immediate goals to fit into the host country's long-range plans. If the multinational recognizes this social responsibility and shapes its policies accordingly, it can hope that the host country will recognize a mutual benefit to its government and to its citizens and that a favorable long-run relationship will result.

Awareness of the host country's social and economic agenda is derived from the research and negotiations that take place prior to the multinational's admission to do business in that country. The enterprise should also recognize that its needs to consciously promote a mutual awareness that its interests and its host's interests will prosper when it acts in a socially responsive manner. Otherwise, it may become a specific and vulnerable target for criticism or even takeover. The multinational enterprise, therefore, must obey local laws and be aware of and respect the cultural and ethical values of the host nation. Additionally, the firm should work cooperatively with the locals to solve problems as they happen.

Political Risk

As business enterprises expand into world markets, they become involved with political systems of varying degrees of stability. Hence, the possibility always exists that changes within these systems may affect the ultimate conduct of the business. This is referred to as *political risk*. For example, when Quaddafi took over in Libya in 1969, the announced goal of the new regime was to reduce foreign influence in that country. Foreign investors were faced, therefore, with eventual changes in the business environment that would affect their profits and other goals of their business ventures. (The next chapter discusses the takeover of a foreign investment by a host government.)

Political Insurance

In international business situations, the political risks are many; for example, war, embargo, license cancellation, conversion of foreign earnings, nationalization, and expropriation. Investors sometimes seek to mitigate the uncertainties of losses in these situations by obtaining political risk insurance.

The Overseas Private Investment Corporation (OPIC) was created to assist U.S. investors and business firms in acquiring political risk insurance when investing in the lesser-developed countries. OPIC is authorized to issue up to $75 billion in investment insurance; no more than 10 percent is available to any one investor. Ordinarily, coverage is limited to 90 percent of a proposed investment, and the premium is based upon the value of the project. As an "agency of the United States," OPIC is under the policy guidance of, and its obligations are backed by the full faith and credit of, the U.S. government. It only insures projects in countries that have signed bilateral investment guaranty treaties with the United States, in which the signatories agree to recognize the rights of each other in the subrogation of claims arising out of investment disputes. Investment proposals must first be approved by OPIC and then approved in advance by the government of the host country. Finally, to be eligible for coverage, each investment proposal must be new or amount to a significant expansion, modernization, or development of an existing enterprise.

OPIC requires that before a loss claim will be honored, the investor must take all reasonable action to exhaust local remedies to prevent or contest conversion or expropriation situations within the host country. Furthermore, the investor must negotiate in good faith with the host country over compensation for seized property. Losses due to war, revolution, or insurrection are covered if the acts complained of are committed by organized forces.

SUMMARY

Since international business is conducted between different countries, a business enterprise will have foreign linkages. The business must be linked to some nation for the purposes of jurisdiction and the establishment of a forum appropriate to the resolution of any legal disputes. Linkage is usually accomplished by reference to the nationality of owners and management.

The business activity of the multinational enterprise is a foreign extension of its domestic business. Transactions take place between persons and business firms; that is, business activities involve sales from manufacturers and intermediaries to consumers, with profit, for the most part, the motive behind each transaction. However, since its international activities take place within the broad dimensions of the international environment, there are factors not present in the domestic situation. History, politics, law, social responsibility, and culture play a significant role in the conduct of international business activities. The decision maker needs to have a fundamental grasp of these different factors to function effectively as a world trader.

The activities of the sovereign state and its impact on business will be analyzed in the next chapter.

SUGGESTED CASE READINGS

Fong Yue Ting v. *U.S. et al.*, 149 U.S. 698 (1893).

Texas Gulf Inc. v. *Canada Development Corp.*, 366 F. Supp 374 (1973).

The El Trifuno Case (U.S. v. *Salvador)*, Arbitration under Protocol of 1901, 1902, For. Rel. U.S. 859.

Sumitomo Shoji America, Inc. v. *Avagliano*, 102 S.Ct. 2374 (1982).

Hellenic Lines Ltd. v. *Rhoditis*, 90 S.Ct. 1731 (1970).

DISCUSSION QUESTIONS

1. The economic goals of the multinational may eventually become political goals. Explain.
2. What are some of the legal and economic variables affecting the policy decision to go multinational?
3. What are the reasons for the evolution of corporate rights in modern commercial treaties?
4. What are some of the attributes of corporate nationality?
5. The multinational is both an agent for change and an agent for control. Explain.

CHAPTER 5

▼

Sovereignty and Sovereign Immunity

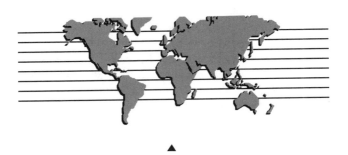

▲

The principle of national sovereignty poses some problems for multinational enterprises. For example, a business firm pursues private goals within geographical areas of its choice, which include the domains of many nations. At the same time, host nations have their public goals, some of which run parallel and others that run contrary to the private goals of the multinational enterprise. Each nation makes agreements with firms and individuals in other nations that will help it attain its national goals. Yet, at the same time, each nation has the sovereign right to abrogate any of these agreements that are deemed no longer in its best interests. Potential investors are therefore concerned about the real risk of losing some or all of their investments because of some overriding national concern of their trading partner. Some questions to be answered prior to investing are: What is the practice of the host nation in terms of expropriation? Does it recognize the obligation to make a "prompt, adequate and effective" compensation? Do the local courts provide adequate remedies to investors who lose their investments?

CHANGES IN PUBLIC POLICY

In direct foreign investment, as in domestic situations, investors look for fair treatment, economic stability, and an opportunity to realize a return on capital. Foreign investors want to avoid or, at least, be protected from the political uncertainties of the host nation that are not present in their home nation. Initially, nations may, as a matter of public policy, attempt to improve their economic development by giving incentives to such foreign investors. Later, however, if these business policies and their implementation by a multinational enterprise adversely affect the nation's ability to compete, technological advancement, political climate, and other aspects of society, governments will attempt to control those activities of the multinational. Sovereign nations have long used controls to increase their share of the benefits generated by multinational enterprises. This is especially true in those developing nations where a dominant nationalistic sentiment sees the economic strength of a foreign business as eroding national sovereignty. The host state views itself as not having complete control of its own economy, or, at least, as having fewer choices over the means for guiding its economy.

Modifications of Agreements

However, basic to a consideration of world trade is how interdependent a nation is and in what ways in its business activities with other nations; that is, how much is a nation bound by the bargain it makes as a world trader. In each nation the scope, composition, and dependence on world business is a continuing concern in formulating both political and business policies. Therefore, whenever a change or crisis, internal or external, arises, a country may desire to renegotiate or even insist, as a matter of its sovereign right, to unilaterally modify or cancel its trade agreements.

Most countries usually make modifications through legislation or renegotiation; but in either case, the changes run contrary to the basic expectations of the multinational enterprise. The multinational will argue that its agreements are in line with the international legal doctrine of *pacta sunt servanda* — "agreements must be kept at all costs." This argument conflicts, however, with the nation's desire for more flexible contractual arrangements. The latter argument is sanctioned by another established international legal principle, *clausa rebus sic stantibus*, which allows revisions of agreements on the basis of a change in circumstances for the contracting parties.

Expropriation

In addition to the ability of the host nation to modify or cancel agreements, it can also expropriate foreign-owned investments. Nations decide to expropriate in order to exercise sovereignty over their natural resources and related economic activities. This act of sovereignty is deemed socially desirable, as is land reform or the exclusion of alien owners. Whatever the reason, expropriation is a political decision made by a nation to further its own ambitions.

Whenever there is a taking, the literature of international law uses such terms as *expropriation, confiscation,* and *nationalization.* Expropriation involves the taking of a foreign-owned property by a host government. When it is done without compensation, it is deemed confiscation, as took place in the takeover of foreign investments in Cuba in 1960. Nationalization is the taking of all activities or properties in a certain sector of the economy, as in the nationalization of the steel industry in Great Britain. Nationalization, therefore, involves a number of expropriations. Whenever there is confiscation, the host government reasonably expects diplomatic protests and even some form of economic retaliation from the multinational's home country. The investor may also attempt to seek redress of its grievances from courts in another jurisdiction.

Compensation for Expropriation

The right of a state to expropriate foreign investments as an aspect of its sovereignty over its natural resources and economic activity is unquestioned. The basic issue in these situations, therefore, is the financial position of the foreign investor regarding the expropriated property. There is an international legal void regarding the resolution of this issue because there is no one view that all major international groupings (capitalist, socialist, and developing states) can adopt.

The United States takes the position that an expropriation meets the minimum standards of international law only if it is accomplished by prompt, adequate, and effective compensation. This duty to justify compensation is constitutionally mandated in Article 1, Section 4, of the U.S. Constitution. The classical international rule of compensation is defined in Resolution 1803 (XVII) on Permanent Sovereignty Over Natural Resources of the General Assembly of the United Nations, adopted December 14, 1962. That resolution states that in expropriation cases, "the owner shall be paid appropriate compensation, in accordance with the rules in force in the State taking such measures in the exercise of its sovereignty and in accordance with international law."

Developing nations, however, generally repudiate the classical principles regarding compensation as not being responsive to their own development needs and goals, because foreign investors are motivated primarily by the maximization of profit. Finally, about thirty new independent states have been formed since the adoption of Resolution 1803 (XVII), and, inasmuch as they did not take part in the formation of the classical principles, they do not regard the rules as binding on them.

Whether a state will make compensation must be considered in the light of four separate approaches to the question:

1. Nationalization requires compensation and that compensation must be adequate, effective, and prompt.

2. The nationalizing state should make some compensation to the foreign investor.

3. No compensation is required because nationalizing states are carrying out economic and social reform, which is a sovereign right. Compensation may frustrate the sovereign right.

4. International law requires equal treatment of citizens and foreigners; hence, the state is not in violation if it does not compensate its own citizens.

Most of the treaties of friendship, commerce, and navigation to which the United States is party contain provisions that protect property owners against confiscation. For example, Article 6 of the United States Treaty with Pakistan on Friendship and Commerce, November 12, 1959 . . . provides:

> . . . Property of national and companies of either Party shall not be taken within the territories of the other Party except for a public purpose, nor shall it be taken without prompt payment of just compensation. . . .

If compensation is made, it is generally less than the "going concern" value of the subsidiary to the foreign investor.

"Creeping" Expropriation

A taking of property may be preceded by a series of actions by host governments that change the rules that were operative when the original business investment was made. This is sometimes referred to as *creeping* expropriation and may take one or more of the following forms:

price controls

import and export restrictions

legislation that affects managerial control over the multinational firm

a change in the value of currency

confiscatory taxation

It should be noted, however, that a change in the rules that merely makes the business less profitable is not in violation of international law. To be confiscatory, any change must deprive the owner of the right to use, enjoy, or dispose of the property within a reasonable time after the adoption of such a change. Ordinarily, treaties do not offer protection from this type of interference beyond the usual nondiscriminatory and other general provisions.

THE ROLE OF THE COURTS

An investor seeking to recoup losses in a foreign court arising out of a taking will confront two international law doctrines: the Act of State Doctrine and the Doctrine of Sovereign Immunity.

The Act of State Doctrine

A foreign investor may find that a claim for investment loss in connection with a confiscation is barred by the Act of State Doctrine. This doctrine is generally invoked to urge a court not to examine the validity of an act of state that results in expropriation. It focuses entirely on the action taken by a state, the so-called "public acts" of government that have been completely executed. If the doctrine is deemed applicable, the court will not fully examine and decide the claim on its merits. The host government is thereby excused as a wrongdoer because the court has decided it is validly exercising its sovereign power. The traditional formulation of the Act of State Doctrine is expressed in *Underhill* v. *Hernandez*, 168 U.S. 250, 252 (1897):

> Every sovereign State is bound to respect the independence of every other sovereign State, and the courts of one country will not sit in judgement on the acts of the government of another done within its own territory. Redress of grievances by reason of such acts must be obtained through the means open to be availed of by sovereign powers as between themselves.

The Act of State Doctrine allows domestic courts to avoid adjudicating disputes that are a matter of international law and in which judicial intervention might have potentially serious ramifications in foreign relations. The doctrine is closely related to the concept of separation of powers. Its proper application depends on the ability of domestic courts to make the distinction between the responsibilities of the judicial and political branches of government in matters concerning foreign affairs. If, however, the judiciary regards the doctrine primarily as a pragmatic way of avoiding conflict with and embarrassment of the executive in foreign affairs, its application in a given case and the resulting judicial decision are subject to changes in foreign policy. A more solid foundation for the Act of State Doctrine is the concept of separation of powers, which makes it less susceptible to political change.

The Doctrine of Sovereign Immunity

The litigation of an entire claim may be precluded by the application of the Doctrine of Sovereign Immunity. This refers to the notion that, according to international law, sovereign states enjoy certain immunities from judicial jurisdiction when they are a party to a legal action. The extent of this immunity is determined by both domestic law and international law. The concept of sovereign immunity calls into question whether the domestic court has jurisdiction over a foreign state at all. It also affects the domestic court's attempts to evaluate the foreign state's conduct. Finally, even if the domestic court should reach a decision, enforcement of the decision is affected by sovereign immunity.

Over the years two conflicting concepts of sovereign immunity have evolved in international law. According to the absolute theory of sovereign immunity, a sovereign cannot, without giving consent, be made to answer in the courts of another nation. According to the restrictive theory of sovereign immunity, the immunity of the sovereign is only applicable to the public acts of the nation but not to its private acts. As a rule, sovereign immunity has been absolute in the following areas:

international administrative acts, such as expulsion of an alien

legislative acts, such as nationalization

acts concerning the armed forces

acts concerning diplomatic activity

public loans

The basic difference between the Act of State and Sovereign Immunity doctrines is that when sovereign immunity applies — i.e., whenever a foreign state, its instrumentality, or its property is to be made a party to litigation — the court has no jurisdiction to hear claims against a foreign sovereign. The Act of State Doctrine, however, merely prohibits courts in other countries from determining the validity of another sovereign's actions. It is basically an issue preclusion device, which may be introduced by any party in the litigation. Therefore, even if the defendant is a private party and adjudication would involve determining the validity of the acts of a foreign state, the Act of State Doctrine determines whether or not a court can assert jurisdiction and decide a case on its merits.

Modifications of the Act of State and Sovereign Immunity Doctrines

The Foreign Sovereign Immunities Act of 1977

The Foreign Sovereign Immunities Act represents an attempt by the United States to codify the restrictive notion of sovereign immunity. The act provides that a "foreign state," which includes "an agency or instrumentality of a foreign state," is not immune when it has "waived its immunity" or when its action concerns "a commercial activity." "Commercial activity" is defined as either a regular course of commercial conduct or a particular commercial transaction. The purpose of the transaction is immaterial; for example, a contract intended to exploit a state's natural resources constitutes a commercial activity. The FSIA contains special rules for obtaining jurisdiction and provides that commercial property is not immune from attachment prior to obtaining judgment or in order to secure satisfaction of judgment.

The Hickenlooper Amendment

In *Banco Nacional de Cuba* v. *Sabbatino*, 376 U.S. 398 (1964), the Supreme Court held that the judicial branch will not examine the validity of a foreign sovereign government's taking of a property within its own territory so long as the government is extant and recognized by this country at the time of suit and no treaty or other unambiguous agreement regarding controlling legal principles exists. This would be the Court's position even if the complaint alleges that the taking violates customary international law. In the *Sabbatino* case, there was no statement from the executive that exercise of jurisdiction by the Court would interfere with the conduct of foreign policy. In *Bernstein* v. *N.V. Nederlandsch Amerikaansche Stoomvaart-Maatschappij*, 376 U.S. 398 (1964), the Court's refusal to rule on the validity of the expropriation, invoking the Act of State Doctrine, was based on the executive branch's reluctance to have it interfere with the conduct of foreign policy.

The Hickenlooper or *Sabbatino* Amendment to the Foreign Assistance Act of 1964 was the first legislative attempt to limit the scope of the Act of State Doctrine. It was introduced in the Senate in April 1964, less than one month after the Supreme Court decided the *Sabbatino* case. The amendment forbade courts to apply the Act of State Doctrine in any case where a foreign sovereign's acts were alleged to be contrary to international law. Before passing this bill, Congress significantly narrowed its scope to expropriation cases only.

The express purposes of the Hickenlooper Amendment was to overrule *Sabbatino* and to reverse the presumption that courts should automatically apply the Act of State Doctrine to cases questioning the validity of a foreign government's acts. The amendment, in effect, directs the courts not to decline jurisdiction on the grounds of the Act of State Doctrine and to make a determination on the merits according to principles of international law. In all cases, the question of whether the foreign sovereign may claim immunity from legislative jurisdiction must be considered by the court.

The Hickenlooper Amendment was first considered in the *Sabbatino* case on remand from the Supreme Court. The Second Circuit Court of Appeals held that the Hickenlooper Amendment was constitutional and that it prohibited application of the Act of State Doctrine in that case, thus legitimizing the Hickenlooper Amendment as an exception to the Act of State Doctrine. The Supreme Court denied *certiorari*, leaving the Court of Appeals' decision intact.

Two later cases, however, virtually eliminated the Hickenlooper Amendment as a viable exception to the Act of State Doctrine. In *French* v. *Banco National de Cuba*, 242 N.E.2d 704 (N.Y. 1968), the New York Court of Appeals distinguished contractual rights from "rights in property" and went on to hold that the Hickenlooper Amendment did not apply. In other words, the court held that Cuba had merely breached a contract with the plaintiff that was not a "confiscation or other taking" within the meaning of that term in the Hickenlooper Amendment.

The Second Circuit Court of Appeals in *Banco National de Cuba* v. *First National Bank of New York*, 431 F.2d 392 (2d Cir. 1970) held that expropriated property must find its way into the United States if the Hickenlooper Amendment is to apply. This condition severely limits the usefulness of the amendment in that expropriated property rarely appears in the United States. Even when it does end up here, it is likely to have changed hands many times, making the owner of such property nearly impossible to identify.

Alternative Remedies in Expropriation Cases

There are alternatives to adjudicating expropriation disputes that are far more effective and that present fewer legal problems. Wider use of these alternative methods would obviate the need for other act of state and sovereign immunity legislation.

Arbitration

Arbitration is a viable alternative to adjudication. If a foreign investment involves a government contract, arbitration clauses may be negotiable. Such clauses are common in contracts made between many U.S. companies and foreign governments. It may also be possible for parties to submit their disputes to arbitration by an agreement made subsequent to an expropriation.

Negotiation

Disputes involving the proper amount of compensation to be awarded, once an expropriation has occurred, may sometimes be negotiated directly or by third-party representatives.

Expropriation Insurance

The best alternative to adjudication for American investors in foreign countries is expropriation insurance. Expropriation insurance is available from private sources or from the government. The Overseas Private Investment Corporation (OPIC) is a corporate agency of the government designed to provide federally guaranteed insurance against the risk of foreign expropriation to U.S. investors abroad (see Chapter 4).

SUMMARY

Investors, when making a decision to do business in a foreign country, are understandably concerned about the security of their investment. They should be aware that expropriation is a distinct possibility in some nations and that they might not have access to a legal system to recover their losses.

The Act of State Doctrine interacts with the Doctrine of Sovereign Immunity as an international principle of judicial restraint. For example, if an investor sues for the value of property expropriated by a foreign government, a court will not examine the validity of the expropriation if the Act of State Doctrine is found applicable. The assumption will be that the expropriation is valid. The Act of State Doctrine focuses on an action taken by a state and its applicability to the litigation. The Doctrine of Sovereign Immunity applies only when a foreign state is sought as a party to litigation or where its property is involved.

Presently, there is a continuously growing body of case law that distinguishes between sovereign and commercial acts and that interprets sovereign immunity restrictively. The purpose of the restrictive interpretation is to try to accommodate the interest of world traders doing business with foreign governments in having their legal rights determined by the courts. At the same time, the foreign governments must be free to perform certain political acts without having to defend these actions in court.

The next chapter will look into the various aspects of world trade policy.

SUGGESTED CASE READINGS

Underhill v. *Hernandez*, 168 U.S. 250 (1897).

Hunt et al. v. Mobil Oil Corp. et al., 550 F.2d 68 (1977).

Texas Trading v. *Fed. Republic of Nigeria*, 647 F.2d 300 (1981).

Banco Nacional de Cuba v. *Farr*, 243 F. Supp. 957 (1968).

The "Gul Djmel", 204 U.S. 90 (1974)

DISCUSSION QUESTIONS

1. Explain how the concept of sovereignty may bring about change in the investment decisions of the multinational enterprise.
2. Distinguish among expropriation, confiscation, and nationalization.
3. Explain the classical rule for compensation and why developing nations do not consider themselves bound by it.
4. What is creeping expropriation?
5. Distinguish between the doctrines of Act of State and Sovereign Immunity.

CHAPTER 6

▼

World Trade Policy

The purpose of trade among the free-market nations in the world is to increase economic growth. Trade is dominated by the theory of "specialization" according to "comparative advantages." This means that world trade allows economic growth to progress beyond what any nation could achieve through the exploitation of its own resources in domestic markets no matter whether the nation is rich or poor, developed or developing, free market or nonmarket. For the theory of comparative advantages to work, however, there can be no price distortion in the market. The General Agreement on Tariffs and Trade is intended to preserve this free market and to avoid factors that produce distortion, such as tariffs and nontariff barriers.

Comparative advantage does not work in the nonmarket nations because their purpose of foreign trade is simply to export surpluses and to use the foreign currency obtained thereby to pay for imports. The cornerstone of the nonmarket nation's trading policy is that the state has an absolute monopoly on world trade, which is conducted exclusively through state organizations whose function it is to implement "the plan." Pricing, therefore, does not depend on market factors; hence, there is no correlation between domestic pricing, intersocialist pricing, and foreign nonsocialist pricing. Prices are distorted, artificial, and arbitrary.

Formulating a comprehensive policy for a nation's world trade relations must be an ongoing process. Ideally, the policy seeks to balance the concept of protection of domestic industries from foreign competition and encouraging freer world trade. It should be noted at this point that nations sometimes adopt trade policies as a political rather than an economic device to attain particular national goals. Trade policy is also a product of attitudes, laws, regulations, and objectives, all of which determine a nation's rules for world trade relations.

All nations exert control over the exporting and importing activities of the multinational enterprise. The controls may be implemented through legislation or be a result of government policy. For example, government subsidies allow a less-efficient exporter to capture foreign markets by being able to sell at a price that does not reflect production costs. As such, subsidies disrupt the comparative advantage of the more-efficient domestic producer. Legislation plays a large role in the activities of businesses within a nation's boundaries. An important aspect of these laws to the multinational enterprise is that they tend to differ somewhat from market to market even though there are a number of laws that generally regulate world trade and uniformity in regulation has not yet been achieved in some less-developed countries.

IMPORT BARRIERS

Tariffs

Tariffs are tools of national economic policy designed to regulate world trade. A tariff is a tax imposed on imported goods before they can be brought into a country. As a rule, there are three types of tariffs, namely, *ad valorem*, specific, and mixed. An *ad valorem* tariff is a percentage of the total value of the imported goods. A specific tariff is a flat charge per unit or quantity of the goods. A mixed tariff is calculated on the basis of a combination of the *ad valorem* and specific tariff concepts. Also, a nation may have a tariff quota, which changes the rate of a tariff depending upon the amount of imports coming in for the year.

Nontariff Trade Barriers

Nontariff trade barriers are made up of government policies and administrative practices that either discriminate against imports or discriminate in favor of exports. Nontariff barriers influence the product, price, marketing, and promotion of goods sold in foreign markets.

Product Regulation

The product is what the consumer receives when making a purchase. The physical aspects of the product will be affected by laws regarding its purity, safety, or performance. For example, foreign automobile manufacturers must meet American motor vehicle safety standards for automobiles exported to the United States, which means that they might have to modify their products to meet the needs of the U.S. market. Countries use product standards, product testing procedures, and product certifications to slow down or even to stop the flow of imports. In practice, however, nations differ as to the strictness of their controls over products. Of concern to the exporter is whether these restrictive factors are compatible with the importing nation's international obligations to pursue freer trade.

Local laws constrain other product features, such as packaging, labeling, and warranty. For example, in some countries the containers in which pharmaceuticals for external application are sold must be manufactured of a certain type of glass and have a certain shape. As a rule, labeling is subject to more legal requirements than packaging. For example, labels might be required to include: the name of the product; the name of the producer or distributor; a description of ingredients or use of product; weight, either net or gross; and country of origin. As to warranty, there is relative freedom to formulate a warranty in all countries. However, code-law countries generally place a stricter product liability on the producer than do common-law countries. This difference would not be reflected in the written warranty but in the legal liability of the producer.

Brand names and trademarks are product attributes that face differing national legal requirements. Most of the industrial nations favor some international uniformity. However, there are differences between code-law countries (ownership by priority in registration of a brand) and common-law countries (ownership by priority in use) in the use of the brand or trademark. One important thing to know is the countries where brand piracy is a problem. Chapter 9 gives extensive coverage to these and other aspects of product policy.

Pricing Regulations

The pricing policies of a multinational in a foreign market will reflect income levels, degree of industrialization, availability of credit, and the presence of foreign and domestic competition. Prices may be lower in one foreign market than in another because costs are lower. However, governments may exercise price-control authority over exports either actively or potentially, and this authority may be applied economywide or limited to certain sectors. For example, price controls may be limited to essential goods to control their export. Also, some countries maintain high prices because of governmental monopoly control of certain resources. Therefore, the effect of these controls on world trade decisions will vary considerably among products and nations.

Marketing Regulations

The multinational enterprise has a high degree of freedom in choosing marketing channels from among those available in a particular market. One of the major legal questions in marketing management is the legality of tying a marketing representative to an exclusive contract to represent one client. Fortunately, this option is allowed in most of the world's markets. In fact, the strongest legal constraint does not apply to firms managing their own marketing in foreign markets but rather to exporters who are selling through distributors or agents — middlemen — in that market.

Promotion Regulations

Advertising is one of the more controversial elements of marketing and is subject to more control than others. Most nations have some laws regulating advertising; in addition, advertising groups in many nations have self-regulatory codes.

Most advertising regulation pertains to the message and its truthfulness. The advertising of certain products may also be controlled because governments consider some products more sensitive than others and therefore restrict their promotion. An indirect restriction is the prohibition of advertising in certain media — for example, some nations allow no cigarette or liquor advertising on television or no commercials at all on radio or TV. Sales promotion techniques encounter greater restriction in some foreign markets than in the United States. In the United States, there is often no constraint on contests, deals, premiums and other sales promotional devices, whereas in foreign markets, premiums may be restricted as to size, value, and nature. For example, free introductory samples may be restricted to one-time usage of the product rather than a week's or month's supply.

Balance of Payments

The myriad of rules and regulations for world trading are also affected by a nation's balance of payments problems. The balance of payments is a system of accounts designed to show how a nation finances its world trade transactions. It is not a measure of the total foreign assets or liabilities that a nation may possess at a given point in time, but it influences world trade policy because it reflects changes that take place in a nation's financial claims on and obligations to the world community. The balance of payments summarizes all government, business, and private business activity that took place with foreign nations during the year. A nation's balance of payments can affect the value of its monetary unit; influence decisions made by the government regarding exports, imports, and the flow of investment funds; and can help determine domestic economic policy.

INTERNATIONAL COOPERATION IN WORLD TRADE

Governments take different approaches to harmonizing their world trade policies with each other. One approach is to periodically review trade policy under the auspices of the General Agreement on Tariffs and Trade (GATT).

GATT

After World War II, the free-world trading partners made an attempt to reduce trade barriers in order to encourage freer trade. In 1948 they met in Havana to complete a draft of the charter for the International Trade Organization (ITO). The United States failed to ratify the ITO treaty, however, and the organization failed. The United States turned instead to the General Agreement on Trade and Tariff (GATT), which had been drafted in Geneva in 1947. Under authority delegated to President Truman in the Reciprocal Trade Agreement Act of 1934, the United States was able to join the Contracting Parties to GATT by executive agreement. The basic concept of GATT is to liberalize world trade. Its main activities fall into three categories: (1) tariff bargaining, (2) quantitative restrictions, and (3) settlement of disputes.

Initially, GATT was not intended to be an international organization but a trade agreement that would embody the results of tariff negotiations. But it has evolved into an international organization that sponsors tariff negotiations, settles disputes, and generally administers the GATT agreement. The basic document mentions only "Contracting Parties" and an "Executive Secretary"; however, a number of committees have evolved over the years. The most important of these is the Council, composed of representatives of member countries who deal with matters between working sessions. The Council meets as needed, exercises advisory powers, and makes up an agenda for each annual session. In addition, there is a Trade and Development Committee; the Balance of Payments Committee; Committee II, an agricultural committee; and the Trade Negotiations Committee.

The general concept of GATT is to establish a basic set of rules under which world trade bargaining can take place. The results of the bargaining will then be incorporated in a draft master agreement that includes not only tariff agreements but also protective clauses to prevent evasion of tariff concessions. GATT has three basic methods of dealing with the abatement of nontariff barriers and the elimination of tariffs and disruptive trade practices:

1. common rules of trade that define "most-favored nation treatment"
2. commitments to observe negotiated concessions and not to initiate restrictive devices
3. special provisions to promote the trade of developing countries

GATT also sets forth a general rule prohibiting the use of quantitative import restrictions such as import quotas. There are, however, four bases for exceptions to this rule:

1. protection of domestic agricultural support systems
2. a balance of payments problem
3. economic development
4. national security

GATT operates through annual meetings where the contracting parties carry on separate negotiations with each of the other contracting parties on a bilateral basis. When a contracting party has completed a series of negotiations, its concessions to each of the other contracting parties are merged into a master agreement. The master agreement represents a contracting party's combined commitment to all other contracting parties. This means that if a country gives a tariff concession to another country, it gives the same concession to all countries that adhere to GATT. The allowable exceptions are

1. Manufactured products from developing countries may be given preferential treatment over manufactured products from industrial nations.
2. Concessions given to other members of a regional trading block do not have to be given to other nations.
3. Nations that discriminate against products from a given nation may not necessarily be given most-favored treatment by the nation whose products are being discriminated against.

GATT does not have a court in which parties may resolve their disputes. Its regulatory function is accomplished by the fact that members are expected to abide by its rules. A number of disputes are resolved by bilateral consultations between the members. However, when a dispute is not settled bilaterally, it may be taken to the council which will appoint a panel to render an advisory opinion. The panel hears the dispute and makes a recommendation to the contracting parties. Should the panel's advice not be followed, the complaining party may suspend its trade obligations with the other party to the dispute.

The Trade Agreements Act of 1979

The conclusion of the Tokyo Round of Multilateral Trade Negotiations (MTN) in 1979 produced a series of new international agreements that, together with GATT, were intended to further reduce worldwide barriers to free trade. The MTN package was negotiated for the United States by the President's representative according to specific congressional authorization granted in the Trade Act of 1974. Congress implemented these new agreements by enacting The Trade Agreements Act of 1979, which became law in January 1980. The new trade agreements covered such items as reciprocal tariff reductions

subsidies and countervailing duties

antidumping duties

technical barriers to trade relations relating to national product standards

government procurement

import licensing

special treatment of developing countries

customs valuation

The Trade Agreements Act contains revisions to the countervailing duty laws and the antidumping laws and procedures for customs valuation. In addition, the act called for a restructuring of the trade functions of the Executive Branch of the United States government.

The administration of the Trade Agreements Act is influenced by the International Trade Commission, an independent agency of the federal government that advises the President on matters concerning the world trade policies of the United States. For example, the ITC makes recommendations to the President about import adjustments, or, in concert with the President, the commission imposes countervailing duties or antidumping measures.

The New Countervailing Duty Statute

A countervailing duty is a tariff levied to raise the price of an import benefiting from an exporting nation's subsidy. The new statute refers to subsidies provided for the manufacture, production, or export of a class or kind of merchandise. However, the exact definition of *subsidy, bounty,* or *grant* according to this statute has significant ramifications for international trade. The 1979 Act states that the term *subsidy* has the same meaning as the terms *bounty* or *grant* and includes the following situations:

> (B) The following domestic subsidies, if provided or required by government action to a specific enterprise or industries, whether publicly or privately owned, and whether paid or bestowed directly or indirectly on the manufacture, production, or export of any class or kind of merchandise:
>
> (i) The provision of capital, loans, or loan guarantees on terms inconsistent with commercial considerations.
>
> (ii) The provision of goods or services at preferential rates.

(iii) The grant of funds or forgiveness of debt to cover operating losses sustained by a specific industry.

(iv) The assumption of any costs or expenses of manufacture, production, or distribution. . . .

The statute has a condition precedent to the levy of a countervailing duty, namely an ITC determination of injury. A material injury to a domestic industry or a material retardation to the establishment of a domestic industry must be demonstrated.

Under the 1979 Act, an administering authority undertakes an investigation of a complaint either on its own or in response to a petition by a private party. If action is warranted, two types of determinations are reached, each in a preliminary and final form. First, within forty-five days of the commencement of the action, the ITC must make the finding of whether there is material injury or retardation of a domestic industry. Within eighty-five days after commencement of the action, but not before the ITC determination, the administering authority must make a preliminary finding as to whether the class of goods at issue is provided with a subsidy. After this determination, sale of the goods in question is suspended, and an order requiring the posting of a bond in the amount of the estimated subsidy is issued by the administering authority. Next, and within seventy-five days of its preliminary determination, the administering authority must make a final determination of the existence and amount of the subsidy. Then the ITC makes its final injury determination. Should both final findings be affirmative, a countervailing duty will be levied equal to the amount of the subsidy.

The New Antidumping Statute

Predatory dumping to capture a share of a market by undercutting domestic competitors is an unfair trade practice in international business law. Dumping consists of charging lower prices in the target market and making up for them by charging higher prices in other markets. Therefore, the dumping prices do not reflect the fair value of the goods.

The process of imposing dumping duties is similar to that of levying a countervailing duty. Investigation is initiated in the same manner, and there are two sets of findings to be made, each in a preliminary and final form. The ITC makes its injury determination, and the administering agency must find out if the goods are being sold for less than fair value (LTFV). Within 160 days of the commencement of the action, but not before the ITC has made its findings, there is a preliminary

LTFV finding. There are provisions for speeding up the determination or granting an extension.

Should the LTFV findings be affirmative, sale of the goods in question is suspended, and the importer must post bond in the amount of the estimated dumping duties. When final determinations are affirmative, a dumping duty equal to the amount by which the foreign value of goods exceeds the U.S. price is assessed and collected. An antidumping duty remains in effect only as long as and to the extent necessary to counteract the dumping that is causing the injury.

Custom's Valuation

The 1979 Act requires that the customs valuation of goods be calculated on the "transaction value" of the imported item. It is "the price actually paid or payable for the merchandise when sold for exportation to the United States" plus "certain amounts reflecting packing costs, commissions paid by the buyer, any assist, royalty or license fee paid by buyer, and any resale, disposal, or use proceeds that accrue to the seller."

The United States Trade Representative

The Trade Agreements Act of 1979 directed the President to propose a restructuring of the international trade functions performed by the Executive Branch and to expand the responsibilities of the Office of Special Representative for Trade Negotiations (STR). The STR is the contact point for persons who desire an investigation of alleged noncompliance with any trade agreement. It also has been the principal vehicle through which trade negotiations have been conducted on behalf of the United States.

In the restructuring proposal submitted by President Carter, the title of STR was changed to the United States Trade Representative (USTR). The proposal assigned the Commerce Department the responsibility for the day-to-day administration of the unfair trade laws, export development programs, and MTN implementation, but the USTR was vested with the responsibility for policy supervision and overall coordination of all three of these areas. Specifically, the USTR is responsible for daily negotiations over specific issues as well as the development of long-term policies and strategies for negotiation. It is this office that is responsible for representing the United States in GATT negotiations, East-West trade agreements, and commodity agreements.

EXPORT BARRIERS

The United States and many Western nations maintain export controls for reasons of national security, to promote foreign policy objectives, to control production and price stability, and to prevent the excessive drain of certain scarce raw materials. These objectives can be more readily attained by quotas than by tariffs. Finally, export restrictions may vary by product or by final destination of the product. The decision in *Czarnikow Ltd.* v. *Centrala Handlu Zagranicznego Rolimpex*, [1979] A.C. 351, stated:

> Export licenses are wholly unlike dog licenses or television licenses which are issued automatically upon the payment of a fee and completion of a form. It is incredible that there should be government intervention of any kind in respect to such licenses. Not so in respect of export licenses. They are normally issued by a department of government and depend upon government policy — which alters from time to time. The department concerned may, on behalf of the government, decide not to issue a license or to cancel an issued license, in its own discretion, or as a result of a decree or direction emanating from the government itself.
>
> United States policy toward export controls is set forth in the Export Administration Act of 1979, which states: It is the policy of the United States to use export controls only after full consideration of the import on the economy of the United States and only to the extent necessary:
>
> (a) to restrict the export of goods and technology that would make a significant contribution to the military potential of any other country . . . which could prove detrimental to the national security of the United States;
>
> (b) to restrict the export of goods and technology where necessary to further significantly the foreign policy of the United States or to fulfill its declared international obligations; and
>
> (c) to restrict the export of goods where necessary to protect the domestic economy from the excessive drain of scarce materials and to reduce the serious inflationary impact of foreign demand.

Under the 1979 Act, the President is authorized to "curtail or prohibit the exportation of any goods, technology, or other information subject to the jurisdiction of the United States." For the statute to apply to an export transaction, either the goods or the persons involved must be "subject to the jurisdiction of the United States." This would include foreign subsidiaries of U.S. companies. The act seems to limit the power of the President to goods still within the United States. Also, the act charges the secretary of commerce to maintain a "commodity control list" of goods, technology, or countries subject to import controls that exporters may consult in advance of exporting.

Export controls are administered primarily by the issuance of a license by the secretary of commerce. The act provides that a license may be

> general — one that does not require approval, a general permission to export
>
> qualified general — one that authorizes multiple exports and requires an approved application
>
> validated — one that authorizes a specific export, issued after an approved application

Enforcement of the license requirement takes place at the point of export. It is the responsibility of customs' personnel to make certain that an exporter presents a Shipper's Export Declaration of what is being exported along with satisfactory evidence of an export license. A willful violation of the act may result in imprisonment for not more than ten years and a fine of $250,000 or five times the value of the export, or $1,000,000, whichever sum is higher. It should be pointed out that no license is required to export goods to U.S. territories and possessions or for most exports to Canada.

SUMMARY

All the nations of the world exert extensive control over their trading activities with other nations. It is this fact that most markedly distinguishes world trade from domestic.

There will always be conflict over how a nation uses its resources, who will control their use, and how the economic benefits will be shared between the local citizen and the foreign resident. Under U.S. law freedom to export is a privilege, not a right. For this reason the export of commodities, services, and technology is controlled by a system of export licenses.

Nationalism plays a significant role in shaping a nation's policy toward the multinational enterprise, as is the case whenever the multinational is used as a tool for economic growth. However, the multinational enterprise should be aware of the fact that nations sometimes employ political devices to attain economic goals, which may or may not always be in the best interests of the multinational enterprise.

The next chapter will examine the basic documents used to facilitate world trade activities.

SUGGESTED CASE READINGS

Western Stamping Corp. v. *U.S.*, 417 F.2d 316 (1969).

Bercut-Vandervourt & Co. v. *U.S.*, 151 F. Supp. 942 (1957).

Zenith Radio Corp. v. *U.S.*, 98 S.Ct. 2441 (1978).

K.S.B. Tech. Sales v. *New Jersey*, 381 A.2d 774 (1977).

Klebers & Co. v. *U.S.*, 91 F.2d 332 (1933).

DISCUSSION QUESTIONS

1. What is the theory of comparative advantage as applied to world trade?
2. What is the difference between a tariff and nontariff trade barrier?
3. Explain the balance of payments and its influence on world trade policy.
4. GATT has three basic methods of dealing with the abatement of disruptive trade practices. Describe them.
5. How do nations exert controls over exports?

CHAPTER 7

▼

International Contracts

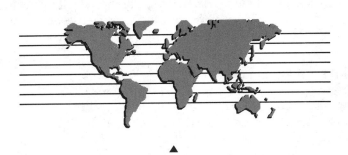

▲

The contract is used to facilitate world trade. It is a legal document created according to a body of domestic law — sometimes more than one body of law — that attaches rights, duties, and obligations to the parties to an agreement. Therefore, reference must be made to those legal systems to determine the legality of the agreement, the rights of the parties, and possible remedies for disputes. Contracts will be treated differently in different legal, cultural, and economic systems.

As the primary document in an export transaction, the contract details the transaction from implementation through to resolution of any possible disputes. Domestic courts generally allow the parties to an international contract to choose the law that governs the transaction and the forum that will resolve disputes. The export transaction is likely to involve more than one contract, however. Contracts for insurance, letters of credit, and transportation, as well as bills of lading, insurance policies, and invoices may all be required. In the international contract, the delivery of shipping documents is an essential element in the performance of the contract.

THE CONTRACTUAL CONCEPT

In a market economy, the contract is the result of a process by which a voluntary agreement is made between parties to do or not to do a particular thing. In business, the contract is a tool by which persons establish a set of rules to govern a business transaction. Although agreements rarely break down in practice, the legal system is available to enforce these agreements. In fact, not many deals are made with much regard given to the enforceability of the bargain, since most contracts are carried out to the mutual satisfaction of the parties involved.

The Free-Market Economies

Contract law represents an effort to ensure the free flow of commercial transactions, and so the contractual concept is especially suited to a free-market economy. Its legal system, responsive to society's needs, modifies the rules of contract law to accommodate the business community. For example, because courts are not able to anticipate every type of business transaction, they allow the parties to draw up their own set of rules and contracts as each business situation dictates. Freedom of contract is an integral part of the free-market system.

Early American contract law reflects this concern for individual freedom of decision. The fundamental natural rights expounded by our forefathers included the right to freely and voluntarily enter into a contract. The Constitution includes a contract clause that prohibits state governments from impairing the obligations of contracts. In this way, the Founding Fathers sought to prevent local governments from interfering with individuals in their exercise of free will. A constitutional corollary to this right is the positive duty of the courts to maintain and enforce contracts, since the concept of natural justice also included living up to a bargain.

The Nonmarket Economies

At one time the contractual concept had no place in the nonmarket nations because it was viewed primarily as a capitalistic invention. Today, however, contracts are an important factor in a planned economy. The authorities instruct state-owned enterprises to enter into contracts with each other and dictate many of the terms. A contract holds the state enterprise to "economic accountability" and also measures the success of the overall state economic plan. The contract is thus considered a transaction made in the public interest.

Whenever the overall plan fails, new planning must take place and it takes precedence over existing contracts. Whatever the changes are, they are incorporated into the plan by changing existing contracts. Thus, the manager of a state enterprise under contract to buy goods from another enterprise will be relieved of his or her obligations if changing conditions have made the goods no longer needed.

The Contractual Concept Under Common Law and Civil Law

Both common-law and civil-law countries recognize the enforceability of mutual promises due largely to the requirements imposed by the worldwide expansion of trade. Under civil law, contracts carry with them a number of implicit promises that will be enforced, whereas under common law a promise must be part of the contract to be enforced. The common-law contract is therefore somewhat more detailed than the civil-law contract, which contains fewer pages because many of the contractual conditions are detailed in the code and need not be repeated in the contract. Common-law contracts often spell out definitions, precise relationships, liabilities, and the like, and must contend with such items as the parol evidence rule and the Statute of Frauds.

The two systems also differ in methods of resolving disputes. In common-law systems, judicial opinions are referred to as precedents in subsequent cases. Thus, they influence future decisions and the interpretation of statues. The civil-law courts are not bound by precedent, but they are bound by the provisions of a code of law. The codes are intended to be comprehensive, consistent, and, it is hoped, uniform. Consider the following excerpts from the civil-law codes of West Germany and Russia. The German Civil Code provides at 285: "The debtor is not in default due to delay so long as nonperformance is due to circumstances for which he is not responsible." Article 222 of the RSFSR Civil Code contains the requirement of fault: "A person who fails to perform an obligation or who performs it in an improper manner is financially liable only if fault is present (intent or negligence) except in cases specified by law or by contract. Absence of fault is proven by the person who has breached the obligation."

THE INTERNATIONAL SALES CONTRACT

The international sales contract is drafted to accommodate traders who deal directly with each other. The bargaining sessions cover such items as prices as affected by market forces, risk factors, and terms relating to security of payment. The final agreement represents the private law of a private transaction. In contrast to the usual domestic transaction, performance of international agreements involves greater distances and longer periods of time before the goods are delivered and payment is required. And, as we have seen, international transactions carry a number of unique risks: more than one (1) currency, (2) system of governmental regulation, (3) legal system, (4) language, and (5) set of cultural expectations.

The rights and duties of the buyer and seller in the international transaction vary according to the arrangements they make with respect to the place, time, and method of delivery of the goods and the payment of the purchase price. Despite the distance and time factors and the additional international risks, most of the problems that occur center on performance and the placement of risks. Traders operating in a domestic setting often enter into contracts in a casual manner without considering the contingencies that may occur. International contracts are generally drafted quite carefully and with close attention to the variety of risks that are present. The following provisions are usually included in the international sales contract.

Placement of Risk

Ordinarily, the risk of loss rests with the buyer as soon as the seller delivers the goods to the carrier. The rules regarding risk of loss assume that the requirements of the contract have been correctly followed by the seller.

How the risk of loss rules are interpreted depends upon whether the contract is a shipment contract or a destination-type sales contract. Where the contract calls for "shipment by carrier" and is of the "shipment" type, the risk shifts from the seller on delivery to the carrier. Where the contract calls for "shipment by carrier" to a particular destination, the risk shifts from the seller on tender of the goods by the carrier at the destination point. In all other cases, the seller must "put and hold conforming goods at the buyer's disposition" and give the buyer such notification as necessary.

Shipping Terms

When shipping terms are specified, they determine when the transfer of risk occurs. For example, if an agreement is FOB ("free on board") shipping point, the seller bears the risk of loss or damage until the goods have been delivered to the carrier. If an agreement is FOB destination, the risk is with the seller until the goods reach their destination. The terms C&F or CIF ("cost, insurance, and freight") place an obligation on the seller to ship the goods, to pay insurance and freight charges, and to forward the shipping documents within a reasonable time. In this instance, the risk of loss is with the buyer during shipment of the goods. The use of COD ("collect on delivery") tells the carrier not to deliver the goods until the purchase price is paid. Although the seller retains control over the goods under COD terms, the title passes upon delivery to the carrier. In the case of shipments made on a "to arrive" basis or contracts based on "no arrival, no sale," the seller is not responsible for the goods' failure to arrive if it has not been negligent, but the buyer may avoid the contract. In an ex ship agreement ("from carrying vessel"), the risk of loss does not pass to the buyer until the goods are properly unloaded.

Price

Since the purpose of foreign trade in the free-market nations is dominated by the theory of comparative advantage, there is a realistic price mechanism in contracts. Market forces, such as the costs of raw materials, transportation, production, and marketing, influence pricing in a free market. In the nonmarket nations, pricing depends on a variety of social, economic, and political factors. When the economic plan fails, the foreign trade corporations are directed to purchase goods for export from state factories at domestic wholesale prices and to sell in foreign markets at the best price available. In the case of imports, the directions are the same: buy in foreign markets at the best prices and sell domestically at prices determined by the plan. Therefore, prices are distorted, artificial, and somewhat arbitrary.

Choice of Law and Choice of Forum

All international sales contracts are subject to some system of domestic law. Although many of the basic elements of contract law are the same in all systems, their role and function differ. For example, some mandatory provisions in each domestic system of law will bind the parties and are important in defining such concepts as *force majeure* or impossibility of performance. In nonmarket countries, however, there are two potential problems with enforcing *force majeure* provisions; namely (1) most nonmarket nations do not acknowledge an industrial strike as a *force majeure* event, and (2) most such clauses do not address the problem of nonperformance caused by changes in the economic plan.

In most nations the courts recognize the right of the parties to choose their own applicable law. However, in the absence of an express or implied choice, no one fact or presumption determines applicable law. In nonmarket systems, where the contract was made in most situations governs what system of law applies, usually local law. The U.S. attitude toward choice of forum, choice of law clauses is reflected in *Scherk* v. *Alberto Culver Co.*, 417 U.S. 506 (1974). The court's line of reasoning in this case represents a reversal of some 150 years of previous rulings.

> Such uncertainty will almost inevitably exist with respect to any contract touching two or more countries, each with its own substantive laws and conflict of law rules. A contractual provision specifying in advance the forum in which disputes shall be litigated and the law to be applied is, therefore, an almost indispensable precondition to achievement of the orderliness and predictability essential to any international business transaction. Furthermore, such a provision obviates the danger that a dispute under the agreement might be submitted to a forum hostile to the interests of one of the parties or unfamiliar with the problem area involved.

It should be noted that even though the parties have selected an appropriate system of law to govern their contract, this does not resolve any disputes. The relevant law must still be argued in court.

Breach, Remedy, and Enforcement

In a trading relationship, breach of contract occurs most frequently through conflicting understandings or interpretations of the terms of the contract. In dealings with a nonmarket country, breach is always possible through cancellation. The contract will detail the consequences of breach and the remedies available. All legal systems go along with the parties' agreement on these matters, in the absence of any overriding policy influences brought to bear on the forum. If the breach and remedy clause is not included in the contract or not acceptable to the forum, then the forum will apply its own remedies.

OTHER CONTRACTS USED IN INTERNATIONAL TRADE

The Bill of Lading

When a seller puts goods in the hands of a carrier, a receipt is issued called a *bill of lading*, which is defined as

> . . . a document evidencing the receipt of goods for shipment issued by a person engaged in the business of transporting or forwarding goods and includes an airbill. "Airbill" means a document serving for air transportation as a bill of lading does for marine or rail transportation, and includes an air consignment note or air waybill. [U.C.C. 1-201(b).]

The bill of lading is a contract between the carrier and the shipper of goods that covers the terms and conditions of the arrangement between them. It acknowledges the carrier's receipt of the goods, it describes the quality and condition of the goods, it is signed by the carrier, and it states the terms of transport and delivery of the goods including an agreed-upon destination. The purpose of the bill of lading is to enable the owner of the goods to dispose of them easily, even though they are not in his or her physical possession. While the goods are in transit, for example, the seller is able to pledge the goods with a bank or sell them to a buyer.

A straight bill of lading specifies the name of the person to whom the goods are to be delivered. The carrier is contractually obligated to deliver the goods to that person only. However, if the bill of lading is negotiable, the carrier undertakes to deliver the goods not to a named person but to the holder of the bill. In the case of a negotiable bill, the carrier is obligated to take up and cancel the bill upon delivery of the goods. A clean bill of lading, as used in international trade, depends on general port custom at the loading port. According to the U.S. Supreme Court in *St. Johns N.F. Shipping Corp.* v. *S.A. Companhia Geral Commercial Do Rio De Janeiro*, 263 U.S. 119 (1923), where there is no such custom and the contract is silent on the matter, the clean bill of lading means "under deck storage." Therefore, carrying the goods on the deck is a violation of the contract.

The International Letter of Credit

The letter of credit facilitated the growth of world trade because traders can use it to minimize risk while meeting their financial obligations. A letter of credit is a written communication from a bank to an exporter in which the bank agrees to pay for goods upon presentation of an invoice for goods shipped to the bank's customer, the buyer. Thus, the seller does not run the risk of not getting paid and having to go to a foreign jurisdiction to pursue the claim. In effect, the letter of credit allows the credit of a bank to be substituted for that of the buyer.

Revocability

Whether the letter of credit is a firm commitment or whether it can be revoked is, as a rule, generally left to the courts to decide in light of the facts of the case and general law, with due regard to the usual course of dealing and usage of trade. To avoid problems, the exporter should make certain that a letter of credit clearly states that it is irrevocable. If the letter is silent on this matter, the exporter is in a predicament if the issuer revokes the letter while the goods are en route.

Confirmed or Advised Credit

The terms of the letter of credit specify whether credit must be confirmed by a bank in the exporter's country or whether the issuing bank is only advising that credit has been extended. If the exporter is the holder of a confirmed letter of credit, that means that a local bank is obligated to the extent of its confirmation of the letter whenever the exporter submits a bill of lading and an invoice for the goods. With a letter of credit that is only advised by a foreign bank, the exporter is relying on the credit of a bank about which nothing is known. The advising bank is not required to honor drafts or demand for payment made under the letter of credit. The bank has only advised the exporter that it is established and that it is under no obligation except to act as an intermediary.

The Actual Transaction

The letter of credit transaction consists of three separate and distinct contracts:

1. the agreement between the bank and its customer detailing the terms by which the bank issues the letter of credit
2. the letter itself, containing the promises of the issuing bank to the exporter
3. the sales contract

It should be noted that the promise of the issuing bank to the exporter is independent of the sales contract and that this promise is the primary obligation of the issuing bank.

THE U.N. CONVENTION ON CONTRACTS FOR THE INTERNATIONAL SALE OF GOODS

The vast growth of world trade in recent years has increased the need to make commercial law more uniform. The United Nations' Convention on Contracts for the International Sale of Goods (CISG) represents a major contribution to the attempts to resolve this problem. The CISG reflects the realities of world trade, such as the crossing of legal and ideological boundaries, the differences in common- and civil-law systems, the different economies of the world, and the different stages of development of the various nations of the world.

The Convention governs the formation of contracts for the sale of goods between parties whose places of business are in different countries when (a) the states are signatories to the Convention; or (b) the conflict-of-laws rule in the forum countries calls for the application of the law of a signatory country. It applies to "the formation of the contract of sale and the rights and obligations of the seller and the buyer arising from such a contract," but not to "the validity of the contract or any of its provisions or of any usage." The Convention recognizes freedom of contract and allows the parties to "exclude the application of this Convention." Where gaps exist in the Convention's provisions, they are to be filled "in conformity with the general principles on which [the Convention] is based or, in the absence of such principles, in conformity with the law applicable by virtue of the rules of private international law." The Convention does not apply to consumer sales or to product liability.

Article 23 of the Convention provides that a contract "is concluded at the moment when an acceptance of an offer becomes effective in accordance with" the Convention's other rules. This formality is mitigated by provisions that make practices between the parties and trade usages relevant in the determination of the parties' intent to enter into a contract. Whether there is an acceptance depends on the interpretation of parties' statements and other conduct. The Convention provides that "due consideration is to be given to all relevant circumstances of the case including the negotiations, any practices which the parties have established between themselves, usages and any subsequent conduct of the parties." Thus, relevant usages of trade my override the provisions of the Convention. In addition, a court has the power, when determining whether a contract was formed, to look outside the rules of formation established by the parties or the marketplace, rules that may be more practical than the provisions of the Convention.

The Offer

Definiteness

An offer is sufficiently definite under Article 14 of the Convention if it "indicates the goods and expressly or implicitly fixes or makes provision for determining the quantity and the price." The offeror must "indicate the goods" but need not specifically identify the goods in the contract. In a requirements contract, for example, the seller may agree to furnish to the buyer "all of buyer's requirements of a specific good." Under such a contract, the specific goods may not exist at the time of contracting; nevertheless, the goods are "indicated" and a contract has been formed. Under the Convention quantity and price terms must be "expressly or implicitly fix[ed]." The offer need not quote a price as long as a price is "implicit."

Revocation

Under Article 16(1), "until a contract is concluded an offer may be revoked if the revocation reaches the offeree before he has dispatched an acceptance." This post-box rule gives the offeree "a dependable basis for his decision whether to accept." The offeree can generally be sure that dispatch of an acceptance will bind the offeror to the contract since dispatch will terminate the offeror's power to revoke. Article 16(2) provides further limitations on the offeror's power to revoke:

> [A]n offer cannot be revoked:
> (a) if it indicates, whether by stating a fixed time for acceptance or otherwise, that it is irrevocable; or
> (b) if it was reasonable for the offeree to reply on the offer as being irrevocable and the offeree has acted in reliance on the offer.

Acceptance

An "acceptance" under Article 18(1) of the Convention is "[a] statement made by or other conduct of the offeree indicating assent to an offer. Silence or inactivity does not in itself amount to acceptance." Under Article 18(2), an acceptance by return promise "becomes effective at the moment the indication of assent reaches the offeror." Article 21(2) puts a burden on the offeror to inspect a late acceptance to determine whether the cause of its lateness rests with the offeree. If so, the offeror must object or it will find itself bound. Article 18(3) provides that the offeree may bind the offeror to the contract by performing an act without giving any notice to the offeror. The article states that the acceptance is "effective at the moment the act is performed." It is the offeree's reliance, not the communication of notice to the offeror, that creates a contract. Therefore, an acceptance by performance is "effective" at the moment the act is performed. The offeror can avoid this problem entirely by including a provision in the offer that it may not be accepted by performance. A court could also find that the offer required as a condition prompt notification of acceptance.

The Contract

Risk of Loss

Risk of loss passes from seller to buyer at clearly definable moments in the transaction. Under a shipment contract, the risk passes when the goods are handed to the carrier. Under a destination contract, risk passes when the goods are placed at the buyer's disposal. When goods are sold in transit, the risk passes when the contract is made.

Different Terms

In a transaction in which the parties exchange documents that contain different terms, the question arises whether a contract has been formed and, if so, on what terms: the offer's terms, the acceptance's terms, or some combination of the terms in the offer and acceptance. The Convention's basic rule regarding acceptances that change the terms of the offer is stated in Article 19(1): "A reply to an offer which purports to be an acceptance but contains additions, limitations, or other modifications is a rejection of the offer and constitutes a counter-offer." Article 19 applies only if the offeree's reply purports to be an acceptance. Many communications by the offeree will not purport to be an acceptance. For example, the offeree may reject the offer outright or may send a reply indicating that further negotiations should continue. Thus, the offeree can make inquiries concerning the offeror's terms, suggest new terms, or make a counter offer while not rejecting the original offer.

Material Alterations

Under Article 19(2), a purported acceptance will be treated as a rejection and counteroffer in two cases: (1) the offeror objects "without undue delay" to any additions or differences, and (2) the reply contains "material" additions or differences. Subsection (3) of Article 19 gives some guidance as to what constitutes a "material term":

> Additional or different terms relating, among other things, to the price, payment, quality and quantity of the goods, place and time of delivery, extent of one party's liability to the other or the settlement of disputes are considered to alter the terms of the offer materially.

This list of material terms is extensive but not exclusive; the phrase "among other things" makes that clear. But what other terms will a court consider material? What it won't consider material modifications are changes regarding "insignificant matters such as grammatical changes, typographical errors or the specification of detail implicit in the offer"; the offeree is accepting what the offeror intended except for drafting mistakes or stylistic differences.

Breach of Contract

Avoidance

Under the Convention, a buyer or a seller who suffers a breach has the right to specific performance or to "avoidance" of the contract, as well as the right to damages. In the case of nonconforming goods, the buyer may reduce the price. A contract is avoided only when the aggrieved party declares it avoided and gives notice to the other party.

Excuse from Performance

A party is excused from performance in cases of impossibility not reasonably expected. Impossibility includes a breach for impossibility by a subcontractor.

Ratification of the Convention

A country may ratify the Convention with the reservation that it will not be bound by either the section governing formation of the contract or the one governing the sale of goods. Likewise, although under the Convention contracts do not have to be in writing, countries may make an exception in order to retain the requirements of their domestic law. Finally, a country does not have to be bound by the Convention's rule that requires application of the Convention when the conflict-of-laws rule in the forum in question requires application of the law of a country that is a signatory to the Convention. The CISG has been ratified by the U.S. Senate and took effect January 1, 1988, replacing Article 2 of the Uniform Commercial Code in international contracts.

SUMMARY

World traders who contract to sell and buy particular goods create a workable framework for their future business activities with each other. Through negotiations they try to anticipate problems, resolve uncertainties, and allocate responsibilities that will carry them through their contractual relationship.

Every contractual relationship is subject to events unanticipated by the parties that will impact on performance. To the extent that a contract does not anticipate these events and the parties are unable to resolve them, the courts may be called upon to make the necessary adjustments.

International contracts give the parties the power to choose their own applicable law, since more than one legal system may affect the contract. Both the civil-law nations and the common-law nations assign supremacy to the law in the role of a dispute-solving institution. However, the parties to international sales contracts should take into consideration the fundamental differences in attitude towards the law and legal institutions in the other party's society. If world traders understand these differences, they will be less apt to attach a higher judgment value to their own institutions and hence to jeopardize their long-term relationships with their trading partner.

SUGGESTED CASE READINGS

M/S Bremen v. *Zapata Off-Shore Co.*, 92 S.Ct. 197 (1972).

Gaskin v. *Stumm Handel GmBH*, 390 F. Supp. 361 (1975).

Export Ins. Co. v. *Mitsui S.S. Co.*, 274 N.Y.S.2d 977 (1966).

Dixon, Irmaos, & C.I.A. v. *Chase Nat'l. Bank of City of N.Y.*, 144 F.2d 759 (1944).

Boston Ins. Co. et. al. v. *Dehydrating Process Co.*, 204 F.2d 441 (1953).

Transatlantic Financing Corp. v. *U.S.*, 363 F.2d 312 (1966).

Ocean Tramp Tankers Corp. v. *V/O Sovfracht, The Eugenia*, 1964, 2 Q.B. 226.

DISCUSSION QUESTIONS

1. How does the contract facilitate the carrying on of world trade? Explain.
2. Distinguish between the common-law and civil-law systems of contracts.
3. What are some of the purely international risks of contracting?
4. How are the bill of lading and letter of credit used in world trade?
5. What stipulations would be permitted in international contracts and prohibited in domestic contracts?

CHAPTER 8

▼

Business Practices

▲

International business transactions take place within the broad dimensions of an international legal environment that is, in reality, made up of three distinct environments. The first generally consists of the nations of North America, Western Europe, Australia, Japan, and New Zealand. These constitute the capitalist system in which economies rely primarily on private enterprise and the competitive market system. The communist bloc with its centrally planned economies and state-run enterprises makes up the second environment. The central planning system allocates both material and financial resources within these economies. The third environment consists of the so-called developing nations of Asia, Africa, and Latin America. Their economic systems are a combination of many forces and have no clearly defined pattern.

GOVERNMENT POLICY AND INTERNATIONAL TRADE

Fiscal Policy

The international business transaction not only involves the transfer of goods, technology, information, people, and services across international borders but it also involves money. There is no international legal tender for making payments in international transactions. Each nation has a monetary unit that is the common measure of value and the legal medium of exchange within its territory. Only the nation's government can print the bills and mint the coins that can be offered and must be accepted as the usual means for the payment of debt. The issuing of currency must be a government monopoly, and all governments exercise their monopolistic power in the exchange market, that is, the exchange of domestic for foreign currency. It is the exchange rate that creates a possibility of gain or loss in an international transaction. When the exchange rate goes down, domestic money buys more foreign money; when the exchange rate rises, domestic money buys less foreign money.

Inflation poses a basic problem in world trading because it shifts the demand for imports and exports. Inflated costs weaken the competitive position of a trading nation's industries in export markets, while inflated prices stimulate the nation's imports. This puts pressure on the exchange rate, affects the balance of payments position, and, at the same time, increases the possibility of restrictive government action and curtailment of business opportunity. In response to balance of payments problems, governments will utilize financial measures in the world exchange markets, enact domestic fiscal measures, or impose restraints on world trade, all of which impact on the operations of the multinational enterprise. Some nations impose direct controls on foreign exchange transactions, use devaluations of currency, or impose multiple exchange rates for different categories of imports and exports to improve their fiscal position. It is essential for world traders to understand both the causes of and likely governmental reactions to a balance of payments deficit. Those enterprises that are most directly affected by these policies buy and sell in world markets, depend on imported raw materials for production, and are involved in the international flow of capital, such as royalties, fees, dividends, and rentals.

Nonfiscal Trade Barriers

Other national policies also have the potential to affect trade. An obvious example is the interrelation between environmental policy and trade. A legitimate national measure, designed to protect the human environment, may affect imports. Pollution controls on automobiles may in effect proscribe imports from nations whose vehicles do not conform. The Japanese prohibition on the use of certain preservatives in effect imposes an embargo on the importation of certain American agricultural products, which cannot be transported for long distances without such preservatives. But in this instance the matter is complicated by the fact that the danger of these preservatives is debatable and, therefore, the question arises as to whether such national measures are legitimate policies in the national interest or merely disguised trade barriers.

BUSINESS POLICY AND INTERNATIONAL TRADE

Foreign Payoffs

A foreign payoff or foreign payment is a transfer of money or anything of value to foreign officials by a multinational firm in order to secure and protect business investments and/or to facilitate performance of routine duties in a foreign country. There are several different types of questionable foreign payments: aggressive payments, defensive payments, grease payments, and political contributions.

Foreign payments that are classified as aggressive payments include outright bribes paid directly for the purpose of obtaining new business. Such payments, if illegal under the host country's laws, cannot be justified even as a normal business practice. Foreign payments that are classified as defensive payments are made to protect the multinational's existing business operations from adverse sanctions, such as the threat of nationalization or the imposition of a damaging tariff. These payments can be justified if the threats are real and the payment is not for the purpose of obtaining new business. Grease payments are made to minor officials to help expedite a legal action, such as licensing, or to help legal imports through customs. Such payments are considered normal business practice, generally as additional compensation for inadequate salaries. The making of political contributions may not be illegal, depending upon the reason for which they are made and the degree to which they can be justified as an honest exercise of business judgment on the part of corporate management. The question remains, however, whether they are political contributions or aggressive payments or outright bribes.

Many businesspersons defend foreign payments as confidential commissions or normal business practice in certain countries and therefore good business practice. Some individuals claim that they are political contributions and are necessary to defend business interests. Those who defend foreign payments base their arguments on political pressures in host countries where payoffs are intended not to promote sales contracts so much as to deter possible restrictive legislation. Two examples of countries that have restricted foreign ownership are Bolivia (tin) and Chile (copper). Countries such as these need the expertise and the export facilities of the multinational enterprise for the efficient production and sale of their products in world markets. In many countries, however, governments and their established economic and political systems are challenged by growing nationalism, which puts foreign investors in the unenviable status of a "necessary evil." To meet their need for the technical and economic expertise of the multinational, on the one hand, and the nationalistic demand for domestic control of the economy and national resources, on the other, the host country may restrict foreign investment or increase taxes on multinational capital and technology.

Some of the arguments against foreign payoffs are that they (1) conceal an accurate financial picture of the corporation, (2) endanger the credibility of the corporation, (3) enrich individuals rather than the host country, (4) jeopardize the internal operations of the corporation, (5) do not necessarily improve either nation's economic picture, and (6) may jeopardize a nation's foreign policy.

The Foreign Corrupt Practices Act

The U.S. Congress passed the Foreign Corrupt Practices Act in 1977 for the express purpose of prohibiting American firms from bribing foreign officials when seeking overseas business. Because much corrupt activity abroad was concealed through secret foreign bank accounts or through false bookkeeping entries, the Act imposes strict controls on accountants. The Foreign Corrupt Practices Act (FCPA) of 1977 prohibits the making of false entries in books and records of publicly traded companies. It requires that the company's books, records, and accounts accurately and fairly reflect, in reasonable detail, the transactions and dispositions of the company's assets. Since the reliability of the company's books and records depends upon the effectiveness of the company's system of internal accounting controls, the Act also requires that each company devise and maintain a system of internal accounting controls sufficient to provide reasonable assurances that accurate records are being kept. Companies found to have willfully violated the accounting standards provision of the FCPA are subject to fines of not more than $10,000 or imprisonment of not more than five years or both.

The sections of the Act that deal with "foreign corrupt practices" are limited in scope but violations can lead to a fine of up to $1 million. For a payment to constitute a violation five separate criteria must be met: (1) the use of an instrumentality of interstate commerce (such as the telephone or mails) in furtherance of (2) a payment, or even an offer to pay "anything of value" directly or indirectly (3) to any foreign official with discretionary authority or to any foreign political party or foreign political candidate (4) if the purpose of the payment is the "corrupt" one of getting the recipient to act (or refrain from acting) (5) in such a way as to assist the company in obtaining or retaining business for or with, or directing business to, any person. The Act provides that a "foreign official" does not include any government employee whose duties are "essentially ministerial or clerical." Consequently, there is no prohibition against paying substantial sums to minor officials so long as their duties are ministerial or clerical. Such payments are frequently called "grease" or "facilitating" payments and they are made to minor foreign officials to get them to perform customary services that they might refuse to perform, or perform only slowly, in the absence of such payments.

For the payments to be illegal under the Act, the word *corruptly* is used to make clear that the offer, payment, promise, or gift is intended to induce the recipient to misuse his or her official position to wrongfully direct business to the payor or the client or to obtain preferential legislation or regulation. *Corruptly* connotes an evil motive or purpose, but there is no requirement that the payment violate the law of the host country for it to be labeled "corrupt."

BUSINESS PRACTICES: EXPORTING AND IMPORTING

Organizing for Exporting

As a rule, American firms who wish to sell in world markets select one of two methods. One is to sell indirectly through domestic export channels, and the other is to sell directly through the firm's own export department. In the beginning stages of exporting, the firm usually assigns

the task to an independent company. However, if exporting is successful, the firm will become more directly involved.

Indirect Selling

The most widely used indirect export channels are export merchants,
buyers for export, and export agents. Export merchants specialize in
buying goods from suppliers and reselling them in world markets. These
individuals handle all the details and bear all the risks involved in the
transaction. Export merchants are generally employed by smaller firms
who otherwise might not sell directly to world markets. Foreign buyers
generally represent foreign customers, from whom they receive a commission for their purchases. Firms selling to such buyers in these situations usually assume the responsibility for shipping the goods. As a rule,
export agents represent noncompeting suppliers. Sales are made by the
agent in the name of the supplier, who finances and ships the goods.

Direct Selling

Many multinational enterprises sell directly to their world customers.
They establish their own export departments, which either sell directly
to foreign distributors or supervise the firm's own representatives in
world markets. Some of the larger multinational enterprises usually prefer to be represented more directly and establish their own selling outlets
or even assembly and manufacturing plants in foreign countries. Treaties with the host country determine what form of organization, if any,
is allowed in the host country. Generally, the forms that are used are
foreign branches, which are actual divisions of the multinational enterprise and perform the same functions as foreign wholesalers, except that
they are owned by the multinational; and foreign subsidiaries, which
are separate companies wholly owned by the parent multinational but
organized under the laws of the host nation. Often, the product being
sold is shipped in bulk to the foreign subsidiary to be packaged or assem-
bled in the foreign country.

The Distribution Contract

An alternative to indirect and direct export channels is the use of distributors or commission agents to sell in world markets, which is sort of a
middle-ground method of exporting. These individuals possess the
know-how for getting around trade barriers, reconciling differences

among the variety of laws governing world transactions, and handling the commercial and financing requirements of transactions. The distributor and agency relationships relieve the supplier's need to be "present" in other countries.

Distribution contracts must be tailored to the specific situation; however, most agreements have the following basic elements:

the names of the parties and the purposes of the arrangement

the purposes and reasons for any restraints on competition

a definition and description of the product or products to be sold

a definition of the distributor or agent's duties and obligations

a designation of the territory and whether or not the arrangement is exclusive

an exculpatory clause for the supplier's failure to perform

a designation of who pays for advertising and samples

compensation provisions and the currency of payment

the term of the agreement and renewal and termination provisions

provisions for resolving disputes

The terms *agency* and *distributor* have more clearly defined meanings in Europe and other civil-law countries than they do in the common-law countries. The European Economic Community definition of a distributor is that he or she is an individual who assumes the economic and legal risks of his or her own selling activities. The distributor buys goods on his or her own account and attempts to resell them for a profit. The suppliers can provide any necessary technical or financial aid without affecting the legal status of the relationship. An agent, while legally an independent entity, is usually considered an intermediary. In this capacity, the agent obtains business for a supplier in return for a percentage commission. Unlike the distributor, however, the agent does not carry any of the legal or economic risks of the transaction. The agent acts for the interests of the supplier as well as in his or her own interests. The agency relationship is subject to more regulatory control than the distributor relationship. The legal independence or separation from the supplier of both distributors and agents is the basic feature of an indirect sales arrangement. All the member nations of the EEC recognize and accept this independence to a greater or lesser extent.

One of the problems in an indirect selling arrangement concerns the agent's selling of competing products. Agency law provides that an exclusive agent may not deal in competing goods of other suppliers; this obligation does not apply, however, to distributors. The multinational enterprise contemplating an indirect selling arrangement in the EEC should examine the statutory laws of the member nations of the EEC to determine what will happen legally on termination, what can or cannot be done during the term of the arrangement, and to what extent territorial protection and exclusivity can be guaranteed. The fact that the antitrust laws of the EEC do not apply to agency relationships is another consideration. That plus the fact that with an agent a supplier will exercise more control over the pricing or distribution of the product than would be possible with a distributor might make agency preferable to the use of a distributor.

Licensing

Trading technical know-how makes up a significant portion of world trade. The multinational enterprise enters into licensing arrangements to serve a particular market. Every license agreement involves the disclosure and communication of technological know-how, but the multinational enterprise can license its rights in patents, trademarks, copyrights, production processes, and brand names and the company logo without much risk to company assets. Usually, licensing signifies a continuous, close cooperation and mutual confidence, which presumes that the parties will probably enter into more than one contract. Each license situation involves unique considerations, and care must be exercised in drafting each agreement. Clauses included in a license agreement that are likely to create problems include sole, exclusive, or nonexclusive licenses; market limitations; royalty payments; technical assistance; and choice of law.

Sole, Exclusive, or Nonexclusive Licenses   A licensing contract should not rely on the common definitions of *sole, exclusive, and nonexclusive,* but rather should define the terms specifically. Who has the right to use the know-how should not be left to subsequent interpretation. In a sole license, the licensor has agreed to grant a license only to the licensee and to no one else. Under an exclusive arrangement the licensee has the exclusive right, exclusive even as to the licensor unless otherwise provided. The nonexclusive license allows grants of rights to others.

Market Limitations   Licenses must contain clauses indicating the territorial limitations of the licensee's market. Otherwise, licensees are in a position to compete directly in any market against the licensor. In that these provisions are restrictive of competition, they raise some antitrust questions (see Chapter 11).

Royalty Payments   Royalties are payments made to the licensor for the know-how that is the subject of the licensing agreement. The royalty is defined as a given percentage of the net sales price of all licensed products made and used, sold, or otherwise disposed of by the licensee. The payment of royalties is tied into the time period of the agreement. Generally, payments accrue at the time of sale or use, and payment itself is a lump-sum or periodic payment over the life of the agreement. Some nations limit the amount that can be paid annually, either in terms of percentage or lump-sum payments. The royalty clause specifies the currency in which payment is made, so which party is exposed to any foreign exchange risk is clear and who is responsible for converting funds is evident.

Provisions for Technical Assistance   During the period of the arrangement, personnel of the licensee will visit the licensor to acquire the know-how, or personnel of the licensor will visit the licensee to provide expertise or to train the licensee's personnel. Likewise, there will be visits by the licensor to monitor progress under the agreement. The agreement should specify clearly who is to pay for these visits.

Choice of Law   The task of determining which law is applicable to a transaction involving the licensing of technical know-how is complicated by the fact that the transaction covers many considerations and these apply to more than one country. Such transactions raise questions about what the fiscal consequences are of withholding taxes on royalties, what the validity is of the patent that is the subject matter of the licensing agreement, and what the liability is of those persons causing injury and damage while rendering the services required under the agreement. If one tries to take into account all of the various situations that may derive from a licensing agreement, any attempt to define the "proper law" of the contract will appear unreasonable. The terms *applicable law* or *proper law* would seem to be more appropriate to designating the law governing the rights and obligations of the parties.

The parties may choose a law having no connection to their relationship as long as they have a reasonable basis for their choice. For example, parties from a Western European and an Eastern European country may choose Swiss law as a "neutral law" to govern an agreement. The parties may also choose the law that, in their opinion, governs the relationship in the most adequate way. Generally, the law chosen is likely to be that of the country for which the license has been granted; the nationality, if it is the same for both parties; the domicile of one of the parties; or the country where the court to which possible disputes will be submitted is located.

In the absence of effective choice by the parties, the forum to which a dispute is brought will determine the country with which the contract is most closely connected in order to determine the applicable proper law. The country most closely connected is that of the party that performs the "most significant obligation." In license agreements the more "significant" obligation is that of the licensee.

Organizing for Importing

Importing channels, like exporting channels, are either indirect or direct. Indirect importing involves the purchase of foreign goods by American businesses from intermediate organizations that specialize in buying goods from foreign firms. Direct importing is the purchase of foreign goods by American businesses directly from foreign business organizations.

Indirect Importing

Most American business organizations prefer to handle their foreign buying indirectly through import merchants, import commission houses, or import brokers. Import merchants buy from foreign firms with their own money and assume all risks. They may specialize in one or a few products or may import a wide variety of merchandise. Import commission houses receive goods on consignment from foreign business firms and sell the merchandise to American buyers. The import commission house does not take title to goods but in other respects functions very much like the import merchant. Import brokers bring the foreign seller and the American buyer together. They do not take title to merchandise and seldom actually handle it.

The indirect method of importing is popular with American firms because it makes importing convenient; specialized personnel are not needed, since no direct contact is made with the foreign seller; and indirect middlemen are usually Americans, a situation that makes for fewer misunderstandings.

Direct Importing

Most domestic organizations that import directly have an import department and either send buyers to foreign countries or maintain resident buying offices in major foreign trade centers. Resident buying offices buy for one firm or for a group of noncompeting firms, which share the costs of maintaining the overseas offices. In both situations, the American importer handles all details and bears all risks. It must, therefore, have an understanding of the goods being purchased, be familiar with the technicalities of foreign trade, and understand methods of doing business abroad.

THE INTERNATIONAL JOINT BUSINESS VENTURE

The international joint business venture is another way of doing business. It is any form of association required by collaboration over a long period of time between parties from different nations. A long-term construction job in which one party supplies the machinery, management personnel, and technical assistance and the other supplies the land, the labor, and the materials is an example of an international joint business venture. Such arrangements have a variety of patterns. For example, partnerships may be established in which the local investor holds one-half of the shares and the foreign investor holds the other half, or an equity association may be formed in which one partner holds a majority of the shares (though often only 51 percent) and the other partner the minority.

The international joint business venture presents three basic legal problems: (1) Decisions have to be made about what form of organization to choose for the venture in a specific country. For example, the institution of the private company in Great Britain has no parallel in the United States, and the forms available in the common-law and the civil-law systems are substantially different. (2) There are special investment laws and regulations that may limit the participation of foreigners in certain resource industries deemed to be of vital national interest. (3) There are regulations that affect foreign investment directly or indirectly, because the economically underdeveloped countries cannot afford free transfer of currencies or allow imports from abroad to go entirely unregulated.

The Basic Agreement

The basis of a joint business venture is a contract for the protection of a myriad of interests that are affected by the uncertainties of distance and performance. Several basic contract provisions are thus necessary to an agreement: choice of language, choice of law, choice of forum, and provisions concerning government approvals, renegotiation, and stability.

Governing Language

In practice, one language is designated as the controlling one, but appropriate translation will be made for the party not conversant in that language. That language clearly will be one with which the parties are familiar because in the event of a dispute, the language of the contract document is looked to first to determine the rights and obligations of the parties. The language selected is also likely to indicate the parties' intent as to the law to be applied to their agreement. In spite of the controlling language of the document or even of the law chosen by the parties, however, the legal language of the forum can govern de facto. This is because any judicial decision is based on documents, proof, assertions, and reasoning presented in the legal language of the forum. In these circumstances, the governing-language clause is given the effect of a choice-of-law clause in issues of interpretation. For the greatest degree of certainty, the controlling language should also be stipulated for documents relating to the negotiations, execution of the agreement, and any procedural notice requirements.

Choice of Law

The purpose of a choice-of-law clause in a joint business venture contract is to establish certainty. There are situations, however, where any choice of law will be obviated because the circumstances surrounding the agreement dictate the applicable law. This could occur, for example, if the host country requires resolution of disputes according to its laws, a likely event if its government is a venture partner.

The absence of a choice-of-law clause may indicate the parties' inability to agree, but some joint venture parties may prefer not to stipulate any governing law, opting instead to settle any disputes privately. If this proves ineffective, the law governing the contract is inferred from the conduct of the parties and the contract itself. Silence on this matter in the contract is often construed as an assumption that forum law is acceptable to the parties.

When trying to determine their choice of law, parties find severability-of-contract clauses useful. Under this approach, a contract will stipulate the parties' choice of applicable law but will remove one or more specific clauses from its scope. For example, the contract may state that corporate authority to act is determined by the laws of the state of incorporation, not by the stipulated governing law. This segregation of issues is common in agreements between private and international partners. Particular issues may be singled out such as when complying with licensing agreements or obtaining government approvals are made conditions to concluding the agreement. These tasks are then accomplished in conformance with the regulations of the host state.

When the venture is a large project that is to be carried out over an extended period of time, a number of implementing documents, in addition to the basic agreement, are involved: letters of credit, negotiable instruments, invoices, purchase orders, change orders, architects' certificates, and the like. These documents may be closely connected to a number of jurisdictions. For example, the project may require the procurement of goods and services in a number of countries, or shipping and insurance contracts and payments may be required in other places. In this situation, the parties will, even if they make no attempt to control substantive legal issues, negotiate a choice-of-law clause in the basic agreement that stipulates that all documents issued in carrying out the agreement are also to be governed by the law selected.

Choice of Forum

Since rules of conflict are not uniform, choice-of-law clauses are usually complemented by a choice-of-forum selection. The forum does not have to be the one usually associated with the stipulated governing law, nor must the connection among the parties, the transaction, and the forum be more than reasonable. Even the United States has come to approve the parties' choice of a neutral forum.

The choice of forum is generally accepted by both civil- and common-law courts. When the parties attempt to oust other forums that may have concurrent jurisdiction on other bases, such as domicile, however, a more difficult problem may arise. Although the majority of civil-law courts honors such exclusive clauses, as does the United States, they are vulnerable to public policy objections.

Government Approvals

The more common government approvals required may include official authorizations of venture activity at the national, provincial, or municipal level and may entail seeking permission from the appropriate council, ministry, and any foreign exchange institute of the host state. Because approvals are both costly and time-consuming to obtain, responsibility for their acquisition should be specifically assigned in the contract. The agreement is usually held in abeyance and its effective date delayed until such approvals are secured.

Renegotiation and Stability

Renegotiation provisions are typical of large-scale and long-term investment contracts involving natural resources. In such circumstances, the agreement is no longer a creation of the marketplace but an instrument of public policy. As such, the host government may feel free to attempt to change the basic contract on various grounds. To prevent this, many investors insist upon a stipulation-of-stability clause. This clause freezes the essential provisions of the agreement by precluding any legislative or administrative act that would otherwise alter the terms of the agreement or the legal environment of the transaction. Reality, however, dictates that change is a normal feature of international joint business ventures. By providing for periodic renegotiation, therefore, the foreign investor can save the business venture from abrogation or nationalization, especially if changed economic conditions have rendered the agreement patently inequitable.

Notarial Form Requirements

The notarial form requirement is operative in most civil-law countries, whereas it is a practice unknown to the common law. The three major duties of the civil-law notary are: (1) authenticating signatures on private writing, (2) counseling the parties in regard to a transaction, and (3) drafting instruments. The notarial requirement is important to the joint venture participants, for the penalty for noncompliance may be the invalidation of the agreement. Likewise, failure to have secured notarial form is a defense to enforcement of the contract. Some courts, however, will refuse to defeat a contract on "nonsubstantive" grounds as a matter of public policy.

A few jurisdictions waive the notarial form requirement if the contract at issue meets the standards of the place of its execution or of performance. Most jurisdictions, however, are heavily dependent upon the policing capacity of their highly trained notaries and are hostile to foreign notarization. The subject matter of the contract is determinative, for it is the most important type of business transaction that requires the notarial form requirement. It should be noted that securing notarial form is an act separate from obtaining needed government approvals or filing and registering documents with the appropriate government unit.

Since the form serves an evidentiary purpose, it may be wise to have important documents notarized in civil jurisdictions even if there is no legal necessity to do so. The notary's obligation is to set forth the commercial expectations of the parties clearly and concisely, a preventative move that may well be worth the effort should a dispute arise between the parties. In addition, the bureaucratic maze is simplified by the notary's participation and advice, for the notary is often a person in favor with the local government.

SUMMARY

There is no international legal tender for payment in international trade transactions. Each nation controls its monetary unit, which may change in value in response to crisis situations.

Foreign payoffs to obtain overseas sales are a fact of world trade. Some nations encourage them, while others, like the United States, restrict them.

Exporting is the simplest method of engaging in world trade; there are few basic differences between an export sale and a domestic one except that, in the export transaction, one of the parties is dealing in foreign currency. The export enterprise may involve a broker operating on a commission, a wholesale distributor, or an export management company, and the exporting agency may be either an independent entity or a foreign division of a multinational enterprise. Different legal relationships exist between the exporting agency and the export enterprise, depending upon the organizational form of that enterprise.

Licensing provides an entry to foreign markets for enterprises not wishing to invest in a market immediately. It provides a profitable outlet for the controlled sale of technical know-how. Multinational enterprises that export and do not wish to invest in world markets but find themselves constrained by government policy can protect their marketing investments through licensing agreements. For the small enterprise, it is a low-risk method of selling know-how.

Joint ventures are one answer to nationalistic demands by host countries for an ownership share in their own industries. If the right local partner can be found, the venture gains the image of being a partially native firm. The right local partner will provide local capital and reduce the investment risk of the multinational enterprise. Because of its local ties, the venture is also less vulnerable to political fallout.

SUGGESTED CASE READINGS

Oscanyan v. *Winchester Repeating Arms Co.*, 103 U.S. 539 (1881).

Volkswagen International, S.A. v. *Rohlsen*, 360 F.2d 437 (1966).

French v. *Banco Nacional De Cuba*, 242 N.E.2d 704 (1968).

Lehndorff Geneva, Inc. v. *Warren*, 246 N.W.2d 815 (1976).

Clayco Petroleum Corp. v. *Occidental Petroleum Corp.*, 712 F.2d 404 (1983).

DISCUSSION QUESTIONS

1. There are several types of questionable foreign payments — aggressive, defensive, grease, and political. Distinguish among the types.
2. Discuss the arguments for and against foreign payoffs as a condition for doing business.
3. Distinguish between a distributor and an agent.
4. The parties may choose to have a contract governed by a law having no connection to their relationship so long as they have a reasonable basis for their choice. Explain.
5. The international joint business venture presents three basic legal problems. Explain.

CHAPTER 9

▼

The Protection of Property Rights

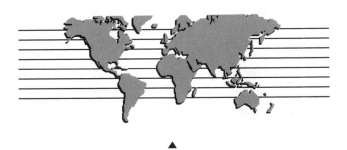

▲

The multinational enterprise owns, sells, and licenses many kinds of intangible assets that require international protection. The most common ways to protect proprietary interests in these assets are through patents, trademarks, and copyrights. In some countries, securing patent and copyright protection is complicated and difficult. In addition, patent and copyright laws vary from nation to nation, which presents a problem for those firms who must protect their rights in many nations. The ownership protection provided by patents, trademarks, and copyrights applies only to situations in which the owner wishes to retain its proprietary rights. Thus there is a distinction between the licensing of technical know-how and an outright sale. In the license situation, the right to use is dictated by the licensing agreement. In a sale, the right to use and other ownership rights pass to the buyer in the agreement. Thus, under a sales agreement the seller cannot control the buyer's use of the property.

In the developing countries, violations of trademarks by local firms are common as is the misappropriation of proprietary brands. Patent violation is less common because patents are used in industrial situations, and these countries are not industrialized enough to make wide use of patented technology. The degree of protection of property rights afforded by any legal system depends upon the ease with which the judiciary is able to take jurisdiction, political pressure, and the time and cost of litigation. For example, a U.S. firm may find it has no legal standing if it is not held "to be in business" in the country where it seeks to bring action. Other factors in a decision to seek redress for violations have to do with the effect of litigation on a continuing business relationship and the ability to enforce a court award.

The following discussion will focus on patents, trademarks, and copyrights. It will examine protection afforded under domestic laws and some of the international agreements that attempt to bring some uniformity to the protection of technical know-how.

TERMINOLOGY

Commercial counterfeiting is the counterfeiting of a brand name of trademarked merchandise. A counterfeit good is, therefore, any good labeled with a false trademark of which the genuine is entitled to protection under the laws of the country of use and is legally registered in the trademark owner's country. Piracy is "the unauthorized duplication for commercial purposes of sound recordings which are then sold in pirate packaging." Knockoffs or palming-off fakes are similar in appearance to the original products but are not sold as genuine articles. Producing knockoffs is not considered an international crime under current trademark statutes. Infringement generally does not occur, therefore, when shipments of Cimega (Omega), Longunes (Longines), and Bulovia (Bulova) watches are sold in world trade. Foreign purchasers who cannot tell the difference between *loom* and *moon* may be wearing "Fruit of the Moon" tee shirts. A related term is *imitation*, which is a copy of an original not sufficiently similar to constitute a counterfeit. A trader in Mexico recently sold local sparkling wine under the same name and label used to identify a premier French champagne but added enough Spanish words so that he was only imitating the product, not counterfeiting.

INTERNATIONAL PATENTING

A patent is a government grant to an inventor of a monopoly over the product, idea, or process that he or she has created. When a business develops a new product for use in a domestic market, it first applies for a domestic patent. Shipping these products or knowledge to other nations raises the possibility that someone will attempt to capitalize on the research done by using the patent without proper authorization. Domestic patents protect the product from infringement only in the nation where it is created, and so patents are registered in each country where the owner wants protection. Although this process is time-consuming and expensive, the basic premise of each country's system is to encourage inventions by giving the inventor a virtual monopoly over his or her invention.

General Considerations

Patent Lifetimes

Patent lifetimes vary among nations, and the date from which the start of the patent life is calculated also differs. For example, in the United States, the life of the patent begins on the date the patent is granted and extends for a period of seventeen years, while in other countries the date the inventor first applies for a patent is the official date.

Prior Description or Use

Some nations allow an inventor to describe the work in an article or commercialize it prior to applying for a patent. Others require that the invention receive its first public exposure through the patent application. There are countries, however, where prior description or commercialization of an invention disqualifies it from receiving a patent.

Obviousness Over Prior Art

Countries vary over the degree to which an invention must be different from prior inventions. For example, in some jurisdictions the new invention must be substantially different from prior art; it cannot be a simple modification of existing technology. Other jurisdictions have no such requirements. Patents may be conferred automatically in some nations, while in others time-consuming searches are conducted to determine whether the invention is different from existing technology.

Publication

In a number of countries, including the United States, a description of an invention is published only after a patent is conferred; in other countries, patents are published within a specified time period following the application for a patent. When the description of an invention is published, competitors are alerted to the activities of the inventor and may begin research to determine how to produce the invention. Consequently, the publication of an invention's description is a significant factor for the inventor, because it is possible for an inventor to file for a patent, have a description of the invention published, and still be denied a patent. The invention is publicly disclosed, and yet the inventor does not obtain patent protection.

Priority

The question of priority arises when two or more inventors file for patents on the same invention at the same time. In most countries, the inventor with the earliest application is awarded the patent. In the United States, patent awards are made on the basis of the date of the actual discovery, not on the basis of the application date. When two or more inventors file for patents of the same invention, therefore, hearings are held in order to determine who first conceived the idea and produced the invention.

Opposition Proceedings

In some countries, descriptions of inventions that are being considered for patenting are published at a given time prior to the conferring of the patent. The public is invited to examine the description of the invention and possibly oppose the grant. These opposition proceedings help ensure that patented inventions are unique and worthy of protection. In nations with opposition proceedings, the courts have a greater tendency to uphold the validity of a patent in any infringement claim than do the courts in those nations who do not provide for them.

Working Requirements

Many countries force the patent holder to exploit the patent. For example, they require that a patent must be "worked" within a specified time or the patent holder to license the technology to someone who is willing to commercialize it. If the technology is not commercialized, the patent is revoked. Working requirements reduce the patenting of trivial inventions and the incidence of defensive patenting.

The Paris Convention

Various attempts have been made to standardize the protection process worldwide. The common goal of these efforts has been a simplified system that makes a single application cover all member countries of a given international agreement. The Paris Convention is the primary international agreement dealing with patents and trademarks.

The International Union for the Protection of Industrial Property, commonly called the "Paris Union," was established in 1883 and last revised in 1971. It is adhered to by the United States and over eighty other countries. The Convention states its goal in Article 1: "The protection of industrial property has as its object patents, utility models, industrial designs, trademarks, service marks, trade names, indications of source or appellations of origin, and the repression of unfair competition."

Under this convention the member nations agree to:

1. Register and protect the trademarks of other member nations to the extent that domestic trademarks are protected.

2. Register trademarks from member states in the form in which they are registered in the country of origin.

3. Acknowledge the protection of property rights without the formality of registration.

4. Grant that an enterprise that files for registration in its native country be given a six-months' priority period to file in a member nation.

INTERNATIONAL TRADEMARKS

A trademark is a name, symbol, figure, letter, word, or mark that distinguishes a good or product from similar goods or products. It identifies the source of the product to which it is attached and endows the product with such attributes as quality, efficiency, and the like. In addition, it gives customers assurance that the product bearing the trademark comes from a common source.

The misappropriation of well-known trademarks generally happens when the trademark owner owns a mark with a worldwide reputation but has not yet obtained a registration or begun use of the mark in the country of the misappropriation. Trademark protection attempts to protect the creative efforts and financial investment of the trademark owner as well as protect consumers from deception in the marketplace. More and more countries are discouraging the growth of domestic industries that rely upon the misappropriation of trademarks. Generally, cases show that trademark rights acquired by international reputation can be protected under certain circumstances. As a rule, the trademark owner must show that he or she has an established reputation in that country, the local infringer has used the trademark in bad faith, and a deception of the public is likely to occur. Obviously, it is better business practice to register a trademark in a country than to have to litigate or buy it back. This might suggest an immediate registration of all of the firm's brands and marks in all countries as an ideal solution. But, although actual registration fees are modest, the total expense of doing this, including legal fees, raises the costs of marketing the product.

Protection of the trademark comes through use in common-law countries or through registration in code-law countries. However, registration follows use in the one, and use must follow registration in the other. In order to meet the use requirements, a product must be sold or manufactured locally. In some instances, the export sale of a few cases of a product is sufficient to establish use for purposes of protection. There is, however, a growing tendency to give protection to trademarks that have not either been used or previously registered in a given country. Protection is afforded in situations where the trademark owner can show an established reputation in a country and that the mark was usurped in bad faith. Where this can be established, confusion in the marketplace is avoided.

The decisions that have granted protection on these grounds have been based on the following circumstances: the international trademark is known in the given country, even in the absence of proven use of the product in that country; or the owner's reputation is generally established through evidence of some minimum contact with the given country. Consider the following excerpt from the case of *Marsin Prunier* v. *Prunier's Restaurant & Cafe, Inc.*, 159 Misc. 551, 288 N.Y.S. 529 (1936):

> With an infinity of names, real and fanciful, from which to choose, the defendants appropriated to themselves the plaintiff's name. That name is not borne by the individual defendants, nor is it claimed to be the name, or anything like it, of any relative of the defendants or

of any officer or employee of either of the defendant corporations. Indeed, it was admitted on the argument that the name was intentionally selected because of plaintiff's well-known reputation and good will which has been built up as the result of decades of honest business effort.

The Madrid Agreement

The 1891 Madrid Agreement Concerning the International Registration of Trademarks provides centralized protection in member states. It requires the registration of trademarks at an International Bureau, which is part of the World Intellectual Property Organization, located in Geneva, Switzerland. Registrations under this agreement are international in that every registration has an effect in several nations and potentially in all member states of the Madrid Union. To take advantage of this agreement, the applicant must be a citizen of, be domiciled in, or have a commercial contact with one of those countries. Also, he or she must first have the mark registered in the national office of that home country. One may then file, through that same national office, an application for international registration.

Once the registration process is completed, the trademark is published by the International Bureau and communicated to the member states in which the applicant wishes to have protection. Each nation, within twelve months from the date on which the mark has been recorded in the international register, has the right to declare that protection cannot be granted to the mark in its territory. The refusal must indicate the grounds for the decision. If a declaration is not made within the one-year period, the international registration has the effect of the national registration.

The international registration continues to depend upon the home country registration for a period of five years. However, a successful attack on the home country registration begun during the first five years results in the invalidation of the international registration, including its national effects. In practice, this seldom occurs because the home country rights are generally the most secure.

The Pan American Convention

Although the Paris Convention has the widest international application to the protection of trademarks, the United States is also a party to other international agreements and treaties. The most notable is the 1929 Pan American Convention (946 State 2907). The Pan American Convention provides that

> Every act or deed contrary to commercial good faith or to the normal honorable development of industrial or business activities should be considered as unfair competition and, therefore, unjust and prohibited.

Article 7 of the Convention gives the owner of a trademark protected in a member country the right to prevent use or registration of an interfering mark in another member country. The owner has the burden of proof that the person using or applying to register the interfering mark has knowledge of the existence and continuous use in any member country of the mark on which the opposition is based. Article 8 protects the owner of a trademark in a member country who seeks registration in another member country when such application is refused due to a previous registration or application for an interfering mark. The original owner may cancel or annul the interfering mark under certain conditions and in accordance with the legal procedures of the country in which the action is brought. The trademark owner must have a prior registration in a member country that predates the application or registration for the interfering trademark. In addition, it must show that the owner of the interfering trademark acted in bad faith in adopting the mark. Alternatively, the original owner must show prior use of the trademark in the country in which cancellation is sought. Article 14 of this convention, which protects trade names without registration, is identical in content to Article 8 of the Paris Convention. Finally, Article 22 provides that goods bearing an unauthorized mark may be seized, if local law permits.

INTERNATIONAL COPYRIGHTS

A copyright is considered a property right from which the holder derives economic returns. It is similar to a patent but it pertains to literary, musical, or artistic works. In Western Europe and in many of the developing nations, copyright statutes include not only basic economic rights but a provision for *dorit moral*, which is known as moral right. The economic aspect of copyright statutes relates to an author's right to prohibit others from copying his or her creation. The moral right allows the author to claim title or paternity to the work and to prevent its alteration or mutilation by others.

Moral right is regarded as being personal to the author and exists throughout the life of the author. As a personal right, it may not be assigned. For example, French law states: "The author shall enjoy the right to respect for his name, his authorship, and his work. This right shall be attached to his person. It shall be perpetual, inalienable, and imprescriptible. It may be transmitted *mortis causa* to the heirs of the authors" (Law No. 57-296 of March 11, 1958, Art. 6). Moral right, therefore, passes to the heirs of the author, or the author may assign the work, or, should the copyright protection expire, the integrity of the work will still be protected by moral right. The concept of moral right includes: the author's right (1) to control publication of his or her work, (2) to have his or her name on that work and not on any other, and (3) to have no changes made without giving consent. Also, the moral right contains the right to not have his or her work be the subject of abusive criticism and the right not to have his or her honor and reputation suffer damage.

A concept related to moral right is that of *droit de suite*, which enables artists to obtain a share in the proceeds from sales of their work. Initially, an artist may sell a work of art for a small sum. Subsequently, if the new owner resells the work for a larger amount, the artist receives nothing. The rationale for *droit de suite* is that an artist's growing reputation may be the reason for the increasing value of the work, and therefore the artist should benefit from these later sales.

France has had a statute regarding *droit de suite* since 1920. The statute provides the artist with a percentage of the sum received by the dealer upon the resale of the work. This amount goes to the creator or heirs during the copyright term plus fifty years. No federal *droit de suite* statute exists in the United States; however, California enacted the California Resale Royalties Act in 1976. This statute provides that when an artist's work is resold for more than $1,000, the artist will receive 5 percent of the amount of the sale, as long as either the sale takes place in California or the seller resides in California. There is no similar provision or statute for authors.

The Berne Convention

The oldest multilateral treaty for the protection of copyright is the Berne Convention for the Protection of Literary and Artistic Works, first signed at Berne in 1886 and last revised in 1971. Countries to which it applies have increased in number from ten to seventy-two and include communist-bloc states, Third World states, and all of the European Economic Community.

The precondition for obtaining protection under this agreement is the first publication (or publication within thirty days of first publication eleswhere) in a member nation. The author need not be a citizen of a member country to enjoy protection under the Convention. Works are "published" when copies are reproduced and made available in sufficient quantities to the public. Examples of works protected are books and other writings, photographic works, works of applied art, and plans and sketches relative to architecture or science. However, protection of works of applied art and industrial designs is limited by legislation in various member countries. Because there is no requirement in this agreement for copies that are visually perceptible, computer software is within the scope of its protection, but the actual scope of protection is determined by the domestic law in each country.

Moral right has been protected by this treaty since the Rome Conference of 1928, at which an Italian proposal to safeguard such rights became Article 6bis. The first clause of Article 6 defines this right as being separate from copyright and as allowing the author to prohibit any modification of the work and to claim paternity. The duration of this right is to be the same as that of copyright, or life plus fifty years, and this right cannot be assigned. The second clause states that the precise conditions of protection will be determined by a particular nation's legislation.

Moral rights under the Berne Union are not given as much protection as they are under some nations' domestic statutes. For example, the Union does not prohibit the destruction of creative works, and protection lasts only as long as the copyright term itself. By contrast, in France, for example, moral right is perpetual, to be safeguarded by heirs. Article 5(1) of the Berne Union provides that "authors shall enjoy, in respect of works for which they are protected under this Convention, in countries of the Union other than the country of origin, the rights which their respective laws do now . . . grant to their nationals, as well as the rights specially granted by this Convention." Thus, an author will receive, at minimum, the protection granted under the moral right section of the treaty as well as the protection of the country in which the work is published, which may be more comprehensive. Protection under the Berne Union alone is, however, much more comprehensive and reliable than the protection provided under the common-law tort or breach-of-contract actions. If a common-law theory protects the moral right aspect of an American work, this protection ends once the author dies.

If a dispute arises between countries that are members of both the Berne Union and the Universal Copyright Convention, the Berne Union governs.

The Berne Union does not require any formalities of notice or registration as a prerequisite of copyright protection. American authors have traditionally obtained copyright protection under the Berne provisions by the "back-door" route of simultaneous publication. Under this provision, if a work is first published within a Berne member nation or is published simultaneously within the United States and a Berne member nation, the work will qualify for protection. Canada, for example, is a member of the Berne Union, and American authors commonly publish simultaneously in Canada in order to be protected under the Union.

The Universal Copyright Convention

The Universal Copyright Convention of 1952 (UCC) is a major multilateral copyright treaty. It was sponsored and is administered by the United Nations Educational Scientific and Cultural Organization (UNESCO). Several nations are parties to both the Berne Convention and the UCC.

An important feature of the UCC is that it provides for "national treatment" for copyright holders of member countries. To receive such treatment, a work must be written either by a citizen or by a resident of a country that is a party to the treaty or be published for the first time in a member country. For example, an American author is entitled to protection against infringement of his or her work in France under the terms of French copyright law, not that of the United States. Or, if computer programs are first given copyright protection in Germany, then publication of the programs in other member countries is protected in Germany, whether or not the other member country recognizes such protection under its domestic law. Thus, the UCC gives the same protection to a foreign work as is given to a work published by a citizen. To receive protection under the UCC, however, authors must comply with their own nation's copyright statutes. A resident of the United States, for example, must comply with United States copyright law to receive protection under the UCC. If a work is not in a form in which it can be visually perceived, it is not "published" under the UCC. Therefore, widespread dissemination of the work may cause it to be considered in the public domain. This, of course, will depend on the laws of the country in which the work is distributed.

The national treatment concept contained in the UCC led to some confusion in those nations that provide moral right protection under domestic law. Nations that consider moral right or *droit de suite* as an element of copyright protection are required to extend this protection to foreign authors whose own nations do not recognize such rights. A U.S. author, therefore, is able to protect his or her moral rights in German courts, when the author would not be able to accomplish the same protection in the United States.

The United States is a party to the UCC but not to the Berne Convention. The Berne Convention has specific provisions regarding works to be protected, the duration of protection, and the elimination of formalities, as well as the protection of moral right. The UCC, however, does not have such specific provisions, except for a minimum period of copyright protection, and does not recognize the moral right. The UCC reduces the number of formalities necessary for copyright protection but does not abolish them, as does the Berne Convention. All that is required presently under the UCC is a simple notice requirement.

U.S. PATENT, TRADEMARK, AND COPYRIGHT LAWS

The Tariff Act of 1930

A patent that is valid in the United States has an important international effect; that is, foreign goods that are under a U.S. product patent can be barred from importation into the United States. This is true even if the goods were produced abroad by a process subject to a U.S. patent. Section 19 USC 1337 codifies Section 337 of the Tariff Act of 1930, as amended, and is simply referred to as "Section 337." It declares as unlawful

> Unfair methods of competition and unfair acts in the importation of articles into the United States, or in their sale by the owner, importer,

consignee, or agent of either, the effect or tendency of which is to destroy or substantially injure an industry, efficiently and economically operated, in the United States or to prevent the establishment of such an industry, or to restrain or monopolize trade and commerce in the United States. . . .

In the majority of cases decided under Section 337, the primary unfair method of competition is the importation of an article that is covered by the claims of a United States patent. The inclusion of patent infringement within the phrase "unfair methods of competition and unfair acts" is a liberal interpretation, but it developed early in the administration of Section 337 and has received judicial and congressional approval. Comparable exclusionary provisions are found in the patent laws of a number of foreign countries.

The ancillary provision, 19 USC 1337a, which is referred to as Section 337a, goes one step further with regard to patents:

The importation for use, sale, or exchange of a product made, produced, processed, or mined under or by means of a process covered by the claims of any unexpired valid United States letters patent, shall have the same status for the purposes of section 1337 of this title as the importation of any product or article covered by the claims of any unexpired valid United States letters patent.

Section 337a refers to what are called *process patents;* this provision is not founded upon the rights granted the inventor by patent law but grants holders of process patents a remedy available only in the context of the import trade and only as a remedy of unfair competition.

The Lanham Act

Protection of a trademark in the United States developed under common law. Unauthorized use, or infringement, of a mark amounted to a tort, sometimes called *passing off* or *unfair competition.* The common-law concept has been supplemented by federal legislation, basically the Lanham Act of 1946, as amended 15 U.S.C.A. 1051-1127. The Act provides that "the term trademark includes any word, name, symbol, or device . . . and used by a manufacturer or merchant to identify his goods and to distinguish them from those manufactured or sold by others."

A trademark duly registered confers upon its owner substantive rights against infringement of the mark. The Act guarantees national treatment for owners from treaty countries and protects the foreign registration of trademarks. Section 42 of the Lanham Act and Section 526 of the Tariff Act of 1930 allow the domestic owner of an American trademark to bar the importation of goods made abroad that bear that mark. Also, such merchandise is subject to seizure.

U.S. Copyright Law

The 1976 revision of the Copyright Act brings the United States closer to the world's view on copyright protection. "Copyright . . . subsists from its creation and . . . endures for a term consisting of the life of the author and fifty years after the author's death." With the term of protection starting at creation, U.S. law is now closer to the Berne Union. The requirements for protection were simplified by the revision. Notice of claim requires three elements: (1) copyright symbol, (2) year of first publication, and (3) name of the owner of the copyright. Also, these elements must be deposited in such a location as to "give reasonable notice of claim of copyright." U.S. law differs from the Berne Union in that there are no preconditions to protection. One of the goals of the 1976 Act was to create a uniform copyright system that would facilitate international copyright transactions. As such, a provision of the 1976 Act preempts any rights under the common law or statutes of a state that are equivalent to copyright and that extend to works within the scope of the federal copyright law.

SUMMARY

The registered patent protects for a specified period of time an invention of "any new and useful process, machine, manufacture, or composition of matter . . ." against all subsequent finders. This protection is limited by the jurisdiction of the granting sovereign. However, the rights held by the owner can be transferred to others by license. The Paris Convention gives assurances to inventors that they will receive national treatment of their interests. Most countries prohibit the importation of goods produced by a patent infringer.

Trademarks identify the source of the products to which they are affixed. The mark assures consumers that the product comes from a common source and may also give assurance of the quality of the product, etc. All countries have a general interest in protecting their citizens from deception caused by trademark infringement. However, they do not have the same concern for foreign investment in trademarks. There is no worldwide system for the protection of the integrity of trademarks. They are territorial in nature. However, a series of treaties have given some uniformity to efforts for solving the problem.

Generally, copyrights are protected internationally under the Berne Convention of 1886 and the Universal Copyright Convention of 1954. In the United States, copyright protection is available to authors to allow them the exclusive right to possess, make, publish, and sell copies of their intellectual productions or authorize others to do so for life plus fifty years.

In the legal environment of international business, the relatively new phenomenon of supernationalism will be discussed in the next chapter.

SUGGESTED CASE READINGS

Vanity Fair Mills v. *T. Eaton Co.*, 234 F.2d 633 (1956).

British Nylon Spinners, Ltd. v. *Imperial Chemical Industries, Ltd.* [1953] 2 All E.R. 780.

Steele v. *Bulova Watch Co.*, 344 U.S. 280, 73 S.Ct. 252 (1952).

Crimi v. *Rutgers Presbyterian Church*, 89 N.Y.S. 2d 813 (1949).

Goldstein v. *California*, 93 S.Ct. 2303 (1973).

Sheraton Corp. of America v. *Sheraton Motels, Ltd.*, 1964 RPC 202.

DISCUSSION QUESTIONS

1. When two or more inventors file for patents on the same invention, who has priority?

2. Many countries require that the patent must be "worked" within a specified time. Explain.

3. How does registration of a trademark protect the owner as well as the consumer?

4. Explain the concept of *droit de suite*.

5. When are artistic works considered published?

CHAPTER 10

▼

Supernationalism

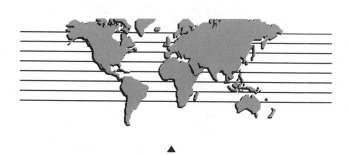

▲

The U.S. Marshall Plan was designed to assist in the economic recovery of Europe after World War II; its success demonstrated the advantages of economic cooperation among countries. In the years following the war, many nations banded together for purposes of economic cooperation with an emphasis on the liberalization of trade. The most successful of these associations has been the European Economic Community, established in 1957. The eventual goal is that economic union will lead to a politically unified Europe. Multinational enterprises that participate in trade with or investment in the European Economic Community must have some knowledge of the operative laws of the community and how its legal system works.

Any organization of a trading union of nations must solve problems relating to the free flow of workers between states, the free flow of capital between states, and the necessity of coordinating the various governmental, fiscal, and monetary policies. In addition, problems caused by diverse economies, political structures, nationalistic sentiments, and the cultural heritage of the states involved must be resolved. Further conflicts arise over the group's competence and power to solve problems and the relationship between the group's common rules and the members' national laws or institutions.

THE CONCEPT OF SUPERNATIONALISM

The concept of supernationalism is based on an agreement to integrate nations having their own geographical areas, economic systems, and political identities into a larger organization with its own political, economic, and legal identity for the purpose of economic, legal, and, potentially, political cooperation. The agreement differs from the more common international agreements, like treaties, which determine the rights and duties of the parties in very limited areas such as tax and trade. It also differs from the traditional international organization, such as GATT, which is confined to imposing rules and processes for decision making and dispute resolution upon its members.

The concept of supernationalism is embodied in an international treaty that creates an institutional structure for implementing the agreement. Of course, before joining such an organization, a nation's government already had the institutions necessary to implement its international agreements. However, supernational status requires the establishment of administrative, executive, legislative, and judicial institutions apart from the corresponding national institutions in the member nations, and, under the concept of supernationalism, sovereign nations must agree to be bound by decisions made by these institutions that are independent of their national control.

THE EUROPEAN ECONOMIC COMMUNITY

The Treaty of Rome

In signing the Treaty of Rome in 1957, six countries (France, Belgium, West Germany, Italy, Luxembourg, and the Netherlands) established the European Economic Community, which is one of the largest established markets in the world. (EEC membership was enlarged to twelve by admission of the United Kingdom, Denmark, and Ireland in the 1970s, Greece in 1981, and Portugal and Spain in 1986.) Through this comprehensive treaty, which contains 248 articles, the members formed a customs union "to ensure the economic and social progress of their countries by common action in eliminating the barriers which divide Europe." Their aim was to create a common market in which goods, capital, people, and business firms would move freely among member states. Creating conditions conducive to this mobility required eliminating various international barriers and neutralizing environmental differences.

The Institutions of the EEC

Normally, the administration of a treaty is handled by the foreign ministries or existing government departments of the countries involved. The Treaty of Rome, however, created separate administrative machinery made up of four main institutions charged with the actual responsibility of implementing policy. The legislative, executive, administrative, and judicial institutions of the EEC are the Commission, the Council of Ministers, the Assembly (European Parliament), and the Court of Justice.

The Commission is the executive body whose function is to ensure that the provisions of the treaty are implemented and to enforce the observance of the treaty by individuals and member states. The Commission also has a legislative function, which is to initiate new policy by making proposals to the Council and to exercise direct rule-making powers. The Commission represents the whole community rather than individual member states.

The Council of Ministers, on the other hand, represents individual national governments. The function of the Council is to coordinate the economic policies of the member states. It is through the Council that national governments influence and control the evolution of the EEC by approving, amending, or rejecting Commission proposals.

In order to carry out their functions, the Council and the Commission have the power to make regulations, issue directives, make decisions, make recommendations, or deliver opinions. Article 189 of the Treaty of Rome makes the following provisions:

> A regulation shall have general applications. It shall be binding in its entirety and directly applicable in all Member States.
>
> A directive shall be binding . . . upon each Member State to which it is addressed, but shall leave to the national authorities the choice of form and methods.
>
> A decision shall be binding in its entirety upon those to whom it is addressed.
>
> Recommendations and opinions shall have no binding force.

The Assembly is made up of representatives from the legislatures of the member states, but it does not enact laws like a true legislative body.

It functions instead in an advisory capacity and thus serves as the arena for the debate of issues. The Commission reports to the Assembly annually, and the Assembly is consulted before certain decisions are made. In practice, the one important power of the Assembly is the right to remove the Commission by a motion of censure passed by a two-thirds majority.

The Court of Justice, made up of eleven judges appointed for six years, passes on the constitutionality of the actions of the Commission and the Council. The judgments of the Court have the force of law throughout the EEC and are binding on individuals, business firms, and national governments. The Court resolves disputes and issues "preliminary rulings" on any question directly referred to it by any court in a member state. The Court seeks to establish uniformity in the understanding, interpretation, and application of community provisions within the member states and to develop the legal process within the community.

Policies of the EEC

The Legal Process

The task of creating a legal process within the EEC is complicated by the fact that community law is economic in nature and by definition is in a constant state of evolution. Therefore, there is an on-going need for adaptation as far as implementation of general rules. Article 215 of the Treaty of Rome and Article 188 of the Treaty establishing the European Atomic Energy Community provide that "in the case of non-contractual liability, the Community shall, in accordance with the general principles common to the laws of the member States, make good any damage caused by its institutions or by its servants in the performance of their duties." These are the only provisions of the treaties establishing the EEC that direct the Court of Justice to apply general principles of law to resolve disputes. These general principles are employed in three ways. First, they are used to interpret the treaties and acts adopted by the institutions of the community to implement the basic treaties. For example, when treaties use technical legal terms derived from the laws of member states, the Court of Justice looks to the laws of member states to interpret those terms. Second, general principles of law are used to fill gaps in the basic treaties or in acts adopted by community institutions. Finally, general principles of law provide a basis for assessing the validity of acts adopted by community institutions. The Court will hold these acts invalid, for example, if they violate general principles of law. However, the Court cannot hold a specific provision of the basic treaties to be invalid on this ground.

The application of general principles of law by the Court is similar to the application of general principles of law by other international courts, such as the Permanent Court of International Justice. As stated above, the Court of Justice applies principles derived from the laws of the member states, whereas international courts claim to apply principles that recognize and enforce "the law of nations." The Court of Justice, therefore, makes a detailed examination of the laws of the member states when forming its decisions. In cases decided by international tribunals, however, the tendency is for the parties and the judges to make sweeping claims that a principle is common to all or most of the "civilized nations" in the world without having to support that claim by citing an authority or by citing the laws of only a few states. By examining the laws of the member states, the Court is able to make detailed surveys of comparative law in a manner that international courts, applying worldwide principles, cannot hope to emulate. In those cases where the Court had simply declared a general principle of law, without citing any authority, it seems probable that the judges have taken national laws into account because the Court is made up of judges from all member states.

Where general legal principles are used as a source of law, the Court applies principles that exist in the majority of the member states, even though such principles are rejected by the laws of other member states. It also pays more attention to the laws of some member states than to those of others, as is evident when the Court uses the terminology of one nation's system in order to describe a principle that is well developed in that system but not in others. The Court may also choose from among the conflicting principles of national laws those that it regards as most progressive. In these cases, a principle is stated in broad and abstract terms in order to transcend differences of detail between national legal systems. In applying these principles to the facts of particular cases, the Court possesses some discretion, for the legal process, since it concerns ever-changing economic conditions, must be a creative and not purely a mechanical process. There is a tendency for these general principles to evolve into judge-made law. For example, after a principle has been applied by the Court in a number of cases, the parties and the Court tend to define the scope of that principle by citing the previous judgments of the Court. It is a possibility, therefore, that the Court may eventually apply a principle that is contrary to the laws of all member states.

The following decision in the case of *Italian Finance Administration* v. *Simmenthal S.P.A.* (Case No. 106-77, 1978 E.C.R. 629) illustrates how the Court views the role of the national laws of member countries in the context of community law.

The main purpose is to ascertain what consequences flow from the direct applicability to a provision of Community law in the event of incompatibility with a subsequent legislative provision of a Member State.

Direct applicability in such circumstances means that the provisions of Community law must be fully and uniformly applied in all the Member States from the date of their entry into force and for so long as they continue in force. These provisions are therefore a direct source of rights and duties for all those affected thereby, whether Member States or individuals, who are parties to legal relationship under Community law. This consequence also concerns any national court whose task it is as an organ of a Member State to protect, in a case within its jurisdiction, the rights conferred upon individuals by Community law.

. . . Indeed, any recognition that national legislative measures which encroach upon the field within which the Community exercises its legislative power or which are otherwise incompatible with the provisions of Community law had any legal effect would amount to a corresponding denial of the effectiveness of obligations undertaken unconditionally and irrevocably by the Member States pursuant to the Treaty and would thus imperil the very foundations of the Community. . . .

It follows from the foregoing that every national court must, in a case within its jurisdiction, apply Community law in its entirety and protect rights which it confers on individuals and must accordingly set aside any provision of national law which may conflict with it, whether prior or subsequent to the Community rule. Accordingly any provision of a national legal system and any legislative, administrative or judicial practice which might impair the effectiveness of Community law by withholding from the national court having jurisdiction to apply such law the power to do everything necessary at the moment of its application to set aside national legislative provisions which might prevent Community rules from having full force and effect are incompatible with those requirements which are the very essence of Community law. . . .

The Free Movement of Goods

The prohibition of customs duties and charges having a restrictive effect on trade between member states and the prohibition of quantitative restrictions and measures having a restrictive effect on such trade are contained in Articles 30–34 of the Treaty of Rome. Quantitative restrictions are defined by the Court as "measures which amount to a total or partial restraint of, according to the circumstances, imports, exports or goods in transit." The Court imposes on member states a positive duty to ease the burden on imports associated with customs clearance and other such practices permitted despite these provisions.

Generally, Articles 30–34 of the treaty are concerned with restrictive measures of a nonfinancial character that relate to goods. Since any such measure has an inherent capacity to restrict imports from, or exports to, another member state, those articles suggest that such activities are, in principle, prohibited. The Court does, however, accept national legislation fixing a price freely chosen by the manufacturer or importer as the maximum permitted sale price for products and that generally has an exclusive internal effect within a state. The suggestion is that restrictive agreements between enterprises in the same member state doing business only in that state are not "capable of affecting trade between Member States" in such a way as to constitute a restrictive agreement. Therefore, in the absence of common rules of the community, it is for member states to make rules regulating the production, distribution, and consumption of a product in their own territory, subject to the condition that they do not amount to an "obstacle to trade between Member States."

Case law suggests that national legislation involving a specific restriction on imports, which puts imports at a disadvantage, is an obstacle to trade. According to Article 3 of European Commission Directive 70/50, measures equally applicable to imports and domestic products are prohibited where imports are precluded or made more difficult to obtain or more costly than domestic products. The Court and the Commission see a restriction of trade in instances where products have to comply not only with the legal requirements of the state of exportation but also with the different marketing requirements of the state of importation. Measures applying only to imports or exports or imposing on them requirements different from those imposed on domestic products are also viewed as restrictive. In effect, Articles 30–34 impose a requirement of material discrimination in situations where a measure equally applicable to imports or exports and domestic products has the effect of favoring the latter. But the wording of Articles 30–34 makes no reference to discrimination of any kind, although there are express references to discrimination in other treaty provisions governing the "four freedoms," that is, the free movement of goods, the free movement of workers, the freedom to provide services, and the free movement of capital. The application of such a broad concept of discrimination may be unsuitable in the context of community law, however, on the ground that member states would be obliged to differentiate between products so as to level off competitive advantages within the community in a manner not conducive to the optimum use of resources.

Specific prohibitions against discrimination are stated in other articles. Article 37(2) not only prohibits introduction of measures contrary to the prohibition of discrimination by state trading monopolies but also the introduction of measures contrary to other provisions governing the free movement of goods. Article 36 permits exceptions to Articles 30–34 on various grounds, including protection of the health and life of humans and animals, protection of industrial and commercial property, and public policy. The Court can, for example, determine whether the characteristics of an imported product or the manner of its marketing is such as to pose a danger to the public health.

Maintaining a Competitive Environment

The Treaty of Rome recognizes that free competition is an essential element of a free and integrated economy and contains rules designed to ensure the maintenance of undistorted competition within the community. The EEC's antitrust policy is limited to trade among the member countries and does not apply to purely domestic trade with nonmember countries. Despite these limitations, the Commission has established a common policy on competition that is an essential element of the success of the goals of a common market.

The EEC's antitrust law is centralized in Articles 85 and 86 of the treaty. Article 85 prohibits "all agreements between undertakings, decisions by associations of undertakings and concerted practices which may affect trade between member states and which have as their object or effect the prevention, restriction, or distortion of competition within the common market or which have this effect." Article 86 expressly prohibits business arrangements that result in an "abuse . . . of a dominant position within the common market." These Articles have been supplemented by additional regulations, Council Regulation 17, adopted in 1973, being the major implementing regulation for Articles 85 and 86.

Article 85 contains a broad prohibition of agreements restraining competition. The article provides several illustrative examples of prohibited restrictive activities, such as price fixing, which are prohibited if the general requirements of the article are established. However, the conduct must have a significant effect on trade between the member states, since section 3 of Article 85 exempts restrictive arrangements that can be justified as beneficial to consumers and, therefore, do not overburden competition.

Article 86 permits the maintenance of a dominant position by one or more enterprises within the community. It prohibits, however, an "abuse" of this dominant position if it affects trade between member states. The mere concentration of the majority of multinational enterprises in one company, through a merger or other arrangements, would not be prohibited. Violation of Article 86 is predicated on three factors; (1) dominant position, (2) abuse of dominant position, and (3) effect on trade.

Dominant Position The standard for a finding of dominant position requires an analysis of the firm's share of the market, calculated in percentages held by the firm. It should be noted, however, that the relevant product market must be properly identified before the market share can be assessed. A product market exists if the product is clearly distinguishable from others in its particular features and if it is not reasonably interchangeable with other products. The interchangeability of a product is measured by whether another product satisfies the same need for the buyer of the product. Finally, the relevant market also includes a geographic aspect because the dominant position must be within the EEC or a substantial part of it.

Once a relevant product market is established, it is necessary to determine whether the firm holds a dominant position in that market. A dominant position is determined by an evaluation of such factors as market share, the firm's relative access to the market, the number of competitors and their market share, the market structure of supply and demand, and the firm's access to capital or technological knowledge.

Abuse of a Dominant Position Abuse of a dominant position is considered to occur when dominant power is exploited, used, or exercised to the detriment of suppliers, purchasers, or consumers. For example, the imposition of unfair purchase or selling prices is prohibited, as is limiting production or markets. Article 86 specifically prohibits the use of tying arrangements by dominant enterprises. A contract between a dominant firm and a customer must not require the customer to purchase other goods or services that are unconnected with the subject matter of the contract; hence, tying these goods to the original contract. Such arrangements deny customers freedom of choice as to the products they purchase and they deny competitors access to the "tied" customer. The issue is whether the dominant firm made use of its position to gain a trading benefit that it would not have had if there had been normal and effective competition in the market. The overall test applied to activities deemed an abuse of dominant position is any use of an activity that has anticompetitive effects, which violates the general objectives of the Treaty of Rome.

Effect on Trade   Article 86 also requires that an activity involving the abuse of a dominant position "affect trade between member states." However, the Commission or the Court may find a dominant position by a firm and an abuse of the dominant position without invoking Article 86. The language of the statute implies that a probable influence on the flow of trade between states is sufficient to satisfy this requirement. Therefore, if the effect of the activity is strictly confined to a single member state, Article 86 will not be applied. But Article 86 will apply even if the activity being curtailed involves the supply of goods to countries outside the community if that transaction has consequences for the competitive structure within the EEC. When an enterprise in a dominant position carries on with nonmember countries in such a way that a competitor within the EEC is likely to be eliminated, this will impact on the competitive structure within the community. The competitive structure is also affected by conduct that not only eliminates a competitor in the market but also has the effect of partitioning national markets, or by an activity that constitutes a threat to the objective of a single market between or among member states.

Section 3 of Article 85 establishes specific exemptions from prohibited activities. For example, if the concerted activity "contributes to improving the production or distribution of goods or to promoting technical or economic progress," an exemption will be granted. Article 85 (3) exemptions can be granted by the Commission to individual enterprises or entire categories of restrictive business arrangements. These EEC exemptions are granted only for a limited time.

The exemption provided by section 3 of Article 85 and the "abuse" concept of Article 86 provide a built-in rule of reason to evaluate business activity. There are no arrangements regarded as unlawful *per se* that undermine the primary goal of EEC antitrust law, which is the promotion of economic development and efficiency through the rational allocation of community resources. The presumption under the EEC rule of reason is that an alleged business activity is legal. Hence, the burden of proof is on the Commission to establish that the conduct has a restrictive effect on trade between the member states or is an abuse of a dominant position. The EEC rule of reason looks beyond the economic impact of the arrangement in question to determine if it is justified by some other long-term community goal.

The Administration of Antitrust Policy

Enforcement of antitrust law is basically an administrative process. Complaints can be filed with the Commission by member states, individuals, enterprises with a legitimate interest, or the Commission itself. In response to a complaint, the Commission must hold a hearing to give the enterprise being investigated a chance to present its views. The Commission can enjoin the arrangement and/or impose periodic fines for such arrangements. If the business enterprise involved is located within a member state, the Commission's remedy is applicable within said member state under the civil enforcement procedures of the state. The Commission's decisions can be appealed to the High Court of Justice.

The EEC has a system of concurrent jurisdiction. Thus, a corporation engaged in an anticompetitive practice faces enforcement under both the EEC articles and the antitrust laws of the member states that are compatible with EEC principles. The Treaty of Rome provides for civil enforcement only against business entities, not individuals. The law permits a private cause of action, which voids the terms of agreements that violate Article 85, and thereby avoids any obligations under an illegal agreement. Otherwise, a private individual cannot bring suit under the articles for damages caused by restrictive business arrangements unless the individual can bring suit under the antitrust law of the member state in which the litigation is initiated.

In the EEC all cartels must register with the Commission, and to become legal they must be granted a dispensation. A failure to register makes any private agreement null and void. In addition, the Commission can impose retroactive penalties on the guilty parties. The Commission's initial antitrust efforts were directed at restrictive agreements among enterprises in sales, marketing, and patents under Article 85. Its first important decision was reached in 1964. In that case the Commission forbade Grundig, a German firm, to operate under an agreement giving a French firm, Consten, the exclusive sales rights to Grundig products in France. In the 1970s the Commission turned its attention to "abuses of dominant position" cases. The most notable decision was to fine United Brands, a U.S. company, $1.2 million for abuse of its dominant position in the community's banana market.

OTHER REGIONAL ASSOCIATIONS

The economic success of the EEC has encouraged other groups of nations to form similar associations. Some have become merely customs unions, while others are free-trade areas. A free-trade area is established when a group of nations abolishes restrictions on mutual trade but allows each state to keep its own restrictions on trade outside the group. An industrial free-trade area allows free trade in industrial products only. Some of these regional associations and their members include:

Andean Common Market: Bolivia, Colombia, Ecuador, Peru, and Venezuela.

Association of South-East Asian Nations (ASEAN): Indonesia, Malaysia, The Philippines, Singapore, Thailand, and Brunei.

Caribbean Common Market: Belize, Grenada, St. Vincent and the Grenadines, St. Lucia, Dominica, Antigua, St. Kitts/Nevis, Monserrat, Trinidad and Tobago, Jamaica, Guyana, and Barbados.

Caribbean Group for Cooperation in Economic Development: Barbados, Belize, Dominican Republic, Guyana, Jamaica, Surinam, Antigua, Dominica, Grenada, Monserrat, St. Kitts/Nevis, St. Lucia, and St. Vincent and the Grenadines.

Central American Common Market: Costa Rica, Guatemala, Honduras, Nicaragua, and El Salvador.

Council for Mutual Economic Assistance (COMECON): the U.S.S.R., Czechoslovakia, East Germany, Hungary, Poland, Romania, Cuba, and Vietnam. Finland is an associate member.

European Free Trade Associations (EFTA): Austria, Finland, Iceland, Norway, Portugal, Sweden, and Switzerland.

Latin American Association for Integration (LAAI): Argentina, Bolivia, Brazil, Chile, Colombia, Ecuador, Paraguay, Peru, Uruguay, and Venezuela.

SUMMARY

Regional trade agreements are certain to continue as an essential element in the international business environment. Such economic integration seeks to eliminte internal trade barriers and remove national restrictions on the free movement of workers, goods, services, and capital among member nations. With the elimination of these internal trade barriers, the scope of the market is enlarged from local to regional. These agreements are obviously an important factor in the business operations of a multinational enterprise. For example, firms that previously exported to an area may find it expedient to bypass a trade barrier by setting up local production plants to serve the entire regional market. The regional grouping of nations will adopt measures or policies that favor the producer from the market area over outside competitors. The multinational enterprise will have to concern itself with the legal environments of not only a domestic legal system and a world legal system but also a supernational legal system. Although the multinational faces many uncertainties and conflicts as to which laws apply, common markets increase its available investment alternatives.

The next chapter will focus on the worldwide regulation of the business activities of the multinational.

SUGGESTED CASE READINGS

Italian Finance Administration v. *Simmenthal S.P.A.*, Case No. 106-77, 1978, E.C.R. 629.

H. P. Bulmer Ltd. v. *Ente Nazionale Energia Elettrica Impresa Gia Della Edison Volta (E.N.E.L.)*, Court of Justice of the European Communities, Case No. 6/64, July 15, 1964.

Firma J. Nold KG v. *Commission*, Court of Justice of the European Communities, Case No. 4/73, May 14, 1974.

Commission v. *The Government of the Republic of Italy*, Court of Justice of the European Communities, Case No. 10/61, February 27, 1962.

DISCUSSION QUESTIONS

1. Discuss the nature of the problems that must be solved in the formation of a trading union of nations.

2. What is the concept of supernationalism based on and how is the concept implemented?

3. Discuss the problems encountered in creating a legal process for the EEC's Court of Justice.

4. What factors must be established to show an Article 86 violation?

5. What is the standard for finding that a firm is in a dominant position in the EEC?

CHAPTER 11

▼

Regulation of Competition

▲

The idea of protecting a free-market economy, while having its historical origins in Europe, has been most intensively pursued in the United States. Therefore it is clear why, considering the political and economic strength of the United States, this legal concept has had international impact. It should be noted, however, that American methods of enforcement are viewed by other countries as excessively aggressive. The wide use of private lawsuits is particularly detested abroad. Ordinary aspects of the American legal system such as liberal pretrial discovery policies, punitive and treble damages, contingency-fee arrangements, and the defendant's role as a witness differ from those of other common- and civil-law systems and are likewise viewed with suspicion. The American jury system, under which jurors serve as the arbiters of facts and control the granting and the amount of money damages, is viewed as inherently biased in favor of the private American plaintiff.

Other countries do not necessarily misunderstand the American notion that promotes private litigation; rather, they resent the fact that the methods of American enforcement are being exported through private parties. Lord Denning, a British justice, expressed this sentiment in *Smith Kline and French Laboratories Ltd.* v. *Bloch* [May 12, 1982, 1980 S. No. 6514 (Transcript: Association) May 13, 1982]:

As a moth is drawn to the light, so is a litigant drawn to the United States. If he can only get his case into their courts, he stands to win a fortune. At no cost to himself and at no risk of having to pay anything to the other side. The lawyers there will conduct the case "on spec" as we say — or on a "contingency fee" as they say. The lawyers will charge the litigant nothing for their services but instead they will take 40 percent of the damages — if they win the case in court — or out of court on a settlement. If they lose, the litigant will have nothing to pay to the other side. The courts in the United States have no such costs deterrent as we have. There is also in the United States a right to trial by jury. These are prone to award fabulous damages. They are notoriously sympathetic and know that the lawyers will take their 40 percent before the plaintiff gets anything. All this means that the defendant can be readily forced into a settlement. The plaintiff holds all the cards.

The parent companies of U.S. multinational enterprises are clearly subject to the antitrust laws of the United States. A question arises, however, over the extent to which these laws apply to their foreign subsidiaries, to their licensing arrangements with foreign firms, and to their purchases of foreign companies; and also, over the extent to which foreign companies operating abroad come under the jurisdiction of the U.S. antitrust laws.

The following analysis will focus on some of the antitrust constraints on multinational enterprises as suggested by court decisions and identify some issues raised by U.S. antitrust policy. Also, this chapter will examine the roles of the Sherman Act and the Clayton Act in promoting an international competitive economy.

ECONOMIC REGULATION AND A COMPETITIVE ECONOMY

When forming policy for a strategy, product, sale, or personnel policy, the multinational enterprise must consider the antitrust implications. Arrangements with suppliers, sales to customers, relationships with competitors, advertising, and pricing are all affected by antitrust regulation. The basic concept of economic regulation is to encourage and maintain a competitive economy. For competition to exist, two or more firms must be selling a similar product, and the two firms must want to compete in a given market. This will give traders realistic choices in the areas of price and production. Competition tends to keep potential areas of economic activity realistically open to new entrants in the marketplace, and, it is hoped, this will make producers, distributors, and sellers dependent upon rather than in control of the forces of supply and demand in the world market.

The primary purpose behind the laws regulating business is to impede those combinations of firms that upset the competitive environment. In the United States in the nineteenth century, anticompetitive relationships took the form of business trusts; in the twentieth century, monopolistic enterprises. Abroad, such relationships take the form of international cartels. Although there are many variations of restrictive business practices, restraints generally are accomplished through horizontal arrangements, vertical arrangements, and mergers.

Horizontal arrangements are agreements between businesses at the same economic level to control a specific aspect of their market, such as price or territory. Sometimes these arrangements are made on the pretext of exchanging patent or trademark rights. Vertical restraints are imposed by the seller on the buyer. These restraints are the result of an agreement to divide markets by enterprises that are under substantially unified ownership or control. The two basic types of vertical restraints are those restricting the distribution of a product and those excluding competing firms from a market. Mergers, the consolidation of two or more business entities into one operation, may increase concentration within a market. Mergers can be horizontal, the merger of corporate competitors, or vertical, the merger of a corporation with its customer or supplier.

Although the form of regulatory legislation varies from country to country, three basic principles are common to all antitrust legislation: it (1) prohibits or regulates, (2) allows exemptions, and (3) penalizes.

The prohibition principles makes restrictive business practices and the acquisition of monopoly power illegal and the dominant position a *per se* violation. The regulatory principle used by most European countries permits restrictive business practices or a dominant market position, but they will impose regulations to prevent any abuses arising from such practices or the gaining of a dominant position.

Most antitrust legislation includes specific exemptions for certain enterprises from the application of the laws. In the United States, for example, farm cooperatives and labor unions are expressly exempted from antitrust laws because of a strong public policy in favor of farm activity and collective bargaining. In some countries, like Japan, exemptions permit expansion of certain domestic industries so that they will be more competitive in the world market.

The third principle of antitrust legislation involves enforcement and penalties. Some antitrust statutes have only civil penalties, while others provide for civil and criminal sanctions. Some penalties are applicable only to the business entity, while others also include sanctions for individuals who violate antitrust laws. The European Economic Community, as we have seen, levies civil penalties only against the corporation.

In the United States, enforcement policy is generally concerned with two types of restraint of competition in foreign commerce: (1) those restraints that deprive the domestic economy of the benefits from imports or entry of foreign firms into production in the United States; and (2) those restraints that seriously bar or restrict exports by American firms. Thus, an American's conduct in world trade is not of antitrust concern unless it is found to have the prohibited consequences for competition in U.S. export, import, or domestic markets. In the majority of countries enforcement of the regulatory laws is the responsibility of administrative agencies with review by the courts. For example, in the United States the Federal Trade Commission (FTC) has primary jurisdiction over the enforcement of the antitrust laws, with appeal to an appellate court. The primary jurisdiction for enforcement in the EEC belongs to the administrative body, the EEC Commission (see Chapter 10), with judicial review only by the High Court of Justice.

One of the questions that must be dealt with in the international legal environment is when it is appropriate for a sovereign state to impose its economic regulatory laws upon business activities that take place in other jurisdictions. For example, the United States has delayed American companies from acquiring facilities in foreign nations, forced businesses to sell their interest in foreign operations, and restricted the entry of goods of foreign cartels in which U.S. firms have participated. Even though such actions have been taken, the enforcement issue is not resolved because the policies from which these firms have been restrained were legal in the countries where the actions occurred. Hence, the extraterritorial effect of antitrust regulations creates risks of conflict among nations. The domestic courts charged with enforcement must therefore be aware of the possibility of interference with the basic sovereign rights of other nations. The following case excerpt discusses the jurisdictional question [*Zenith Radio Corp.*, v. *Matsushita Elec. Indus. Co.*, 494 F. Supp. 1161 (1980)]:

> Much of international law is concerned with delineating the respective jurisdictional sphere of nations. Five principles govern the exercise of jurisdiction by a nation: the territorial principle, by which jurisdiction is based on the place where the offense was committed; the nationality principle, based on the nationality of the offender; the protective principle, which governs conduct which threatens the national security or operation of governmental functions, such as counterfeiting and falsification of official documents; the universality principle, under which the custody of a perpetrator of a crime of universal interest, such as piracy, provides jurisdiction; and the passive personality principle, based on the nationality of the victim. As to jurisdiction over economic regulatory matters, only the territorial principle is applicable. That principle, however, admits of two interpretations. Viewed subjectively, a state may extend its jurisdiction over persons found within its borders who violate its law there. Under what the law styles an "objective interpretation," however, a state has jurisdiction over acts which take effect within its borders, regardless of the location of the actor. It is this objective interpretation of the territorial principle of jurisdiction which has generally been accepted in American case law with respect to the Sherman Act.

U.S. ANTITRUST POLICY

The Sherman Act, enacted in 1890, prohibits monopolistic agreements in restraint of trade. The foundation of United States regulatory laws is built on the basis of sections 1 and 2 of the Act and by a series of case decisions. Later statutes have been enacted to supplement the Sherman Act, namely the Clayton Act, the Robinson-Patman Act, and the Fair Trading Act.

U.S. courts have attempted extraterritorial enforcement of U.S. antitrust laws; most other legal systems generally accept that their jurisdiction does not extend beyond domestic territorial boundaries. In *U.S.* v. *Aluminum Company of America*, 148 F.2d 416 (2d Circ. 1945), Judge Hand stated: "Any state may impose liabilities even upon persons not within its allegiance for conduct outside its borders that has consequences within its borders which the State reprehends." The following discussion will focus on implementation of international antitrust law in the United States through the courts' enforcement of the Sherman Act and the Clayton Act.

The Sherman Act

The purposes of the Sherman Act are to: (1) preserve competition in domestic markets by prohibiting conduct that adversely affects competition in the United States, and (2) preserve American export opportunities against efforts to injure or limit those opportunities by anticompetitive activity. The question is to what extent does the Sherman Act apply to conduct that affects U.S. consumers or that impacts upon export opportunities when such activity occurs beyond our borders? The courts generally accept that the Sherman Act applies to anticompetitive activity where it has a direct and substantial effect on domestic consumers or export opportunities. However, the courts seem to regard anticompetitive conduct that has adverse impact only on consumers in foreign nations as of no concern under the Sherman Act. The latter view promotes American export opportunities and American competitiveness in foreign markets. An objection to jurisdiction based on the Sherman Act is not going to cause a dismissal at the outset of a case. Jurisdiction is a matter for factual inquiry, and so is going to be established by a determination of the restriction's actual effect on commerce. Discovery will therefore be necessary or, perhaps, even a full trial before a ruling on a motion to dismiss can be made. American courts have applied the Sherman Act extraterritorially in most cases because of the link either of nationality of American enterprises or their subsidiaries, or of place, in that one of the basic elements of the offense was committed within the United States.

The applicability of the Sherman Act is based on two lines of reasoning: the *per se* rule and the rule of reason. The fact that a bona fide restraint occurs in the course of an international transaction has nothing whatsoever to do with whether the *per se* rule will be applied. The fundamental question asked is what the essential purpose or the effect of the transaction is? If the purpose is to fix prices or allocate markets, the *per se* rules applies, and the parties are subject to penalty. The rule of reason is more flexible and is designed to balance the procompetitive and anticompetitive aspects of any particular agreement. This rule is applied to most international business activity. If the primary purpose of a business arrangement is to enter a market, to perfect distribution in a foreign country, or to effect a transfer of technology, any restrictions that occur that are not required to effect that purpose are subject to the rule of reason. This distinction is critical in world trade because of the political and other barriers to competition in foreign countries. Factors unique to an international transaction will weigh heavily in any rule-of-reason situation.

Consider the following discussion of a "jurisdictional rule of reason" by the U.S. Supreme Court in *Timberlane Lumber Co.* v. *Bank of America*, N.T. & S.A. 549 F.2d 597 (9th Cir. 1976):

> The elements to be weighed include the degree of conflict with foreign law or policy, the nationality or allegiance of the parties and the locations or principal places of business of corporations, the extent to which enforcement by either state can be expected to achieve compliance, the relative significance of effects on the United States as compared with those elsewhere, the extent to which there is explicit purpose to harm or affect American commerce, the foreseeability of such effect, and the relative importance to the violations charged of conduct within the United States as compared with conduct abroad. A court evaluating these factors should identify the potential degree of conflict if American authority is asserted. A difference in law or policy is one likely sore spot, though one which may not always be present. Nationality is another; though foreign governments may have some concern for the treatment of American citizens and business residing there, they primarily care about their own nations. Having assessed the conflict, the court should then determine whether in the face of it the contracts and interest of the United States are sufficient to support the exercise of extraterritorial jurisdiction.

The Clayton Act

Section 7 of the Clayton Act prohibits acquisitions that may substantially lessen competition. In the international context, does section 7 apply to worldwide acquisitions?

The United States has used section 7 in recent years to stop the acquisition of foreign companies by U.S. firms. In 1964 a U.S. District Court ordered the Schlitz Brewing Company to divest itself of its part ownership of Labatt, the third-largest Canadian brewer, which, in turn, owned the General Brewing Corporation of California. Section 7 applied because the parties engaged in U.S. domestic or foreign commerce, and the effect of the acquisition was to substantially lessen competition in the United States. The substantive law of section 7 addresses three problems: one is horizontal, mergers between competitors; a second is a potential horizontal problem, the elimination of a potential competitor; a third is vertical, the merger between a manufacturer and a distributor.

The horizontal criterion is applied when a foreign firm is present in the United States as a competitor, in which case it is treated just like any other competitor. A merger between two substantial foreign-based competitors, given certain market conditions, is as illegal as domestic mergers. The horizontal criterion against certain mergers is the clearest. The conditions for violation of anticompetitive restraints by mergers involving foreign firms exist when mergers among foreign enterprise owners or those potentially owning a U.S. enterprise affect U.S. commerce through imports or affect U.S. commerce through exports. When horizontal mergers take place, firms may cease to act like competitors and begin to act like collaborators even without express agreements to do so. They may tend to be cooperative in pricing and may follow the leader in their pricing moves. Thus, the market may become noncompetitive. As the firms move from competition to tactic collaboration, they are likely to restrict output and raise prices. Elimination of potential competition is the most common type of problem posed by foreign acquisitions.

A merger case based on elimination of potential competition requires specific market conditions. For such a merger to be in violation, a well-defined market, high entry barriers, high concentration of goods in the hands of a few suppliers, and oligopolistic behavior — interdependent behavior rather than competitive — must exist.

In a vertical merger, a U.S. firm may acquire a foreign firm that is a source of supply. However, a merger producing a significant percentage foreclosure may still not be challenged by the government unless it also produces a horizontal effect. If a source of supply or market outlet is closed off that is critical to the viability of competitors under high entry-barrier conditions and a concentrated level of competition is created, then the merger has a horizontal effect. Competitors are reduced to the point that conditions for interdependence are created.

International Enforcement of
U.S. Antitrust Laws

The Antitrust Division of the U.S. Justice Department is in charge of enforcing antitrust laws. The division therefore operates basically within a prosecutorial framework. However, when dealing with foreign commerce and foreign governments, the Antitrust Division may modify its responsibility to enforce, without losing sight of its charge to assess the legality of business conduct.

As a rule, if the Antitrust Division has reason to believe that a violation of the antitrust laws has occurred and that the necessary documents are located in foreign countries, it will request that the affected company supply the necessary documents. At the same time it will assess the chances of successfully obtaining the necessary information by compulsion. The division also takes into consideration the problems that may arise when many and diverse business firms are involved, as well as the involvement of foreign governments.

Generally, a firm will submit for examination those documents located in the United States. This may diminish the scope of the investigation, or it may even eliminate the need for further action. However, the Antitrust Division must obtain all the information necessary to make an analysis and a decision whether to prosecute. No matter what course the division takes, its investigation is affected by concern over the involvement of foreign governments, which is especially important when the particular commodity in question is consumed in large amounts in the United States. In these situations some factors of international control will exist, some form of an orderly marketing agreement — possibly an international commodity agreement — and, therefore, there will be some involvement by foreign governments. A prime example is the situation created by the formation of an international cartel by the oil-producing nations in an attempt to control the international price for oil. A foreign government may refuse to permit the removal of requested documents, or it may even refuse to permit examination of the documents or the obtaining of evidence through depositions. Civil-law courts are reluctant to permit the use of depositions for obtaining evidence because many civil-law lawyers are unfamiliar with the practice. Even in those countries where consular treaties govern the deposition practice, it is not always clear whether the testimony of non-American citizens can be taken.

DEFENSES TO THE ENFORCEMENT OF U.S. ANTITRUST LAWS

BLocking Statutes

The extraterritorial enforcement of U.S. antitrust laws is directly tied to the extraterritorial discovery of evidence. An antitrust plaintiff eventually is going to request that the defendant produce documents that are outside of the United States. In the United States, so long as a U.S. court has personal jurisdiction over the defendant, it can compel the defendant to produce relevant documents from anywhere in the world. Foreign governments, however, regard the U.S. court's requirement of documents located within the foreign state's territory as an infringement of that state's sovereignty.

Many foreign governments have enacted "blocking statutes" that prohibit persons from complying with such extraterritorial discovery requests at the risk of suffering personal penalties. West German law, for example, recognizes a national interest in extraterritorial discovery restraints in Article pt. v. 98 (2) (Aug. 9, 1957), which states that "this law applies to all restraints of competition which have effect within the territory to which this law applies, even if they are caused from outside the territory to which this law applies." Japanese law (Law No. 54 of 1947 6) forbids international cartels without reservation unless the effect of such an agreement on either domestic or world trade is negligible. The most sweeping foreign blocking statute is the British Protection of Trading Interests Act, which was enacted in 1980 following reaction in the United Kingdom to antitrust litigation in the United States. The Protection of Trading Interests Act provides that if measures are taken or proposed to be taken by another country that would apply to acts outside that country by persons doing business in the United Kingdom and these measures are damaging to British trading interests, the British secretary of state may

1. require persons to give notice to the British government of any requirement imposed by such measures

2. give such persons directions for prohibiting compliance with such a requirement

3. prohibit compliance if the requirement imposed on the person in the United Kingdom by the other country is to produce to the foreign tribunal any commercial document or information not within that country

4. deem treble-damage antitrust judgments unenforceable in the United Kingdom

5. invoke the "clawback" clause that allows the defendant to recover back from the plaintiff that part of the award that exceeds actual compensation.

A conflict occurs in the discovery process when a U.S. court order directing the defendant to make an extraterritorial production of documents meets a foreign blocking order prohibiting the defendant from producing the requested documents. The sanction for noncompliance with the U.S. order may be as severe as the entry of a default judgment against the defendant or adverse findings of fact by the American court. The sanction threatened under the foreign blocking order is often a criminal penalty. In this situation, the U.S. rule is that the party is entitled to some consideration from the U.S. court if he or she makes a good-faith effort to have the blocking order lifted. If a person solicits and obtains the foreign blocking order, however, any right to claim that the foreign action is sovereign compulsion, which relieves the defendant of liability, is forfeited.

Sovereign Compulsion

The doctrine of sovereign compulsion is a defense available to defendants in private actions that makes allowance for relevant international considerations. A necessary condition for this defense is that the foreign law compelled the defendant to violate American antitrust law. U.S. courts do not appear to favor this doctrine, however, and have added a number of qualifications to it. For example, the foreign government action, to constitute a defense, must be true compulsion and not mere endorsement, encouragement, or approval of the private conduct. Case law does not answer the question as to what sanction is sufficient to render a finding of compulsion appropriate. The threat of jail sentences or heavy fines seemingly constitutes a credible compulsion. If the threat is merely that of economic loss, a finding of compulsion is unlikely to be made. The court in *Mannington Mills, Inc.* v. *Congoleum Corp.*, 595 F.2d 1287 (3d Cir. 1979) summarized the defense of sovereign compulsion: "The sovereign compulsion defense is not principally concerned with the validity or legality of the foreign government's order, but rather with whether it compelled the American business to violate American antitrust law. . . . One assisting the defense must establish that the foreign decree was basic and fundamental to the alleged . . . behavior and more than merely peripheral to the overall illegal course of conduct. . . ."

Sovereign Immunity

The concept of sovereign immunity has not been significant in the antitrust area because foreign states are seldom sued for antitrust violations.

Thus far, no suit has attacked a foreign government itself but only the proprietary interests of a foreign government. In *U.S. v. Deutsches Kali-syndikat Gesellschaft*, 31 F.2d 199 (S.D.N.Y. 1929), the United States sued to enjoin the violation of antitrust laws by a French corporation that sold potash within the United States. Although the French government owned the majority of the capital stock, the essentially private corporation could not claim immunity (see Chapter 5).

The Act of State Doctrine

Case decisions suggest that the Act of State Doctrine influences the enforcement of antitrust laws in two important ways. The first essentially concerns the concept of comity, which is based upon the respect of one state for the sovereign acts of another (see Chapter 12). The second involves the concept of separation of powers, in that the refusal to sit in judgment on the validity of or motivation for a foreign government's acts is based on the court's need to avoid interfering with the executive branch's conduct of foreign relations (see Chapter 5). Commercial activities are not clearly recognized as exceptions to the Act of State Doctrine. In antitrust actions, courts tend to separate acts of the private party from those of the sovereign state and to avoid invocation of the doctrine.

The Export Trading Company Act of 1982

Export trading companies (ETC) are those domestic firms that act as middlemen between the firm desiring to sell overseas and the foreign customer. The primary function of this type of business is to obtain orders for the client's goods through selection of markets and channels of distribution and advertising campaigns. The export trading company is a single marketing organization that manages exports for a number of firms or just one company. In some situations, it may handle competing product lines. The export trading company, with its experienced personnel and existing sales and distribution networks, offers the multinational ease of entry into a foreign market.

The U.S. Export Trading Company Act of 1982 was enacted to remove some of the uncertainty from the application of the antitrust laws to the joint efforts of export trading companies. It enables U.S. firms to combine resources or engage in activities in overseas markets that might not be permitted in domestic markets. The Act cannot, however, exempt the applicant from foreign antitrust laws. The Act provides for the creation of an antitrust "certificate of review" that is jointly issued by the Departments of Commerce and Justice. Certification establishes that an ETC's proposed business activities will not be in violation of the antitrust laws. Under the Act, the applicant must disclose:

a description of the nature and places of business

type of product

methods of operation for all the applicant's business activities

a description of all goods and services to be exported under the certificate

the applicant's previous two-year sales figures for all businesses under its control

SUMMARY

U.S. antitrust policy toward multinational enterprises can only be assessed in terms of court decisions, whose general implications are, at best, uncertain because they deal with specific cases and are not generally applicable. Even the significance of a particular case is frequently disputed by antitrust scholars.

There is little doubt that the world business community resents the extension of American antitrust activities into its affairs. This resentment is most obvious when the foreign firm finds itself taking part in American litigation. Likewise, both the public trader and the private trader are upset if the American in their marketplace does not have to act according to local expectations. The process of foreign discovery in international antitrust cases faces foreign objection and resistance to what is seen as an intrusion upon foreign sovereignty by U.S. agencies and U.S. courts. These objections are to be expected because discovery not only interferes with the economic interests of the foreign sovereign but may also interfere with the judicial and political responsibilities of the foreign sovereign.

There is no question that restrictive business practices need to be controlled internationally. For all parties concerned, however, some uniformity must exist in that system in order to avoid conflict among nations and among world traders.

The next chapter deals with the resolution of international legal disputes.

SUGGESTED CASE READINGS

Timberland Lbr. Co. v. *Bank of America, N.T. & S.A.*, 549 F.2d 597 (1976).

U.S. v. *National Lead Co.*, 63 F. Supp 5B (1945).

Timken Roller Bearing Co. v. *U.S.*, 715 S.Ct. 971 (1951).

Interamerican Refining Corp. v. *Texas Maracaibo, Inc.*, 307 F. Supp. 1291 (1970).

Mannington Miles Inc., v. *Congoleum Corp.*, 595 F.2d 1287 (1979).

Todhunter-Mitchell & Co. Ltd. v. *Anheuser-Busch Inc.*, 375 F. Supp. 610 (1978).

DISCUSSION QUESTIONS

1. What are some of the ordinary aspects of the American legal system that differ from other common- and civil-law systems?
2. What are the basic principles common to all antitrust legislation?
3. The Sherman Act's rule of reason applies in evaluating the competitive aspects of world business activity. Explain.
4. The extraterritorial enforcement of U.S. antitrust laws is directly tied to the extraterritorial process of discovery of evidence. What problems does this pose for the antitrust plaintiff?
5. Discuss the defenses available in an international antitrust action.

CHAPTER 12

▼

RESOLVING INTERNATIONAL DISPUTES

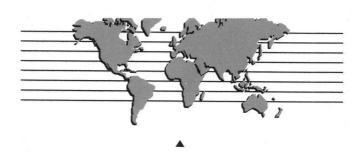

▲

Although everything possible may have been done when negotiating and drafting international business agreements to anticipate and avoid disputes, differences can and do arise in implementing agreements. In the international setting the two basic types of dispute are those over contract rights and duties and those arising from governmental attempts to alter the contract through a change in the operating rules.

The two principal methods for resolving disputes in the international environment are traditional commercial litigation in national courts and international arbitration. Issues such as extraterritorial application of national law, choice of law, and sovereign immunity sometimes limit the usefulness of litigation. Arbitration is therefore seen as an alternative to litigation, not the least because it allows foreign firms to avoid the litigious environment of the United States, where they have a hard time dealing with procedural devices unknown to their legal systems.

FACTORS AFFECTING THE RESOLUTION OF DISPUTES

Employing Legal Counsel

In the face of a constantly changing business environment and the variety of restrictive legal environments, world traders are in constant need of legal expertise in contract negotiations, the preparation of legal documents, and representation before courts and administrative agencies. The first consideration is whether the parties can employ their "home" lawyer. Typically, home lawyers have the status of laypersons in other legal systems. In addition, what is considered legitimate professional activity in a domestic practice may be regulated or even banned in other countries. The ability to practice law is also regulated by immigration and employment statutes deemed applicable by a host state. China has decided not to permit foreign lawyers to practice in China, for example. A recent Chinese law has specified that all lawyers must be Chinese citizens; it does not mention what foreign law firms or individual lawyers may or may not do in China. Other countries regulate the activities of foreign lawyers but few go as far as China's total ban. Some countries impose geographic limits, while others limit foreign lawyers' appearances to certain courts. However, the more liberal host states allow the home lawyer to provide legal advice, draft legal documents, and represent clients in contractual negotiations. Admission to a foreign bar is rarely the solution to the problem due to citizenship and other requirements, such as study at a national university and a period of clerkship. What generally occurs is that the home lawyer will establish a relationship through correspondence with foreign firms that can assist his or her clients on legal matters.

Employing local counsel may be necessary or even, in some situations, highly advisable in establishing and financing a multinational business enterprise. In the case of direct investment in a foreign country this is especially true due to the various restrictions and requirements for approval that must be obtained as a condition for being allowed to do business. Local legal advice is also useful because the means for avoiding or mitigating local rules may vary from one country to another, or because actions legal in one country may be subject to criminal penalty or civil liability in another — lobbying for an exception to a rule, for example, or extending favors, giving gifts, paying commissions to intermediaries, making political contributions, or even paying cash to public officials.

The Exhaustion of Local Remedies Rule

An established rule of international law is that local remedies must be exhausted before a party may resort to international proceedings. Local remedies are considered those available through courts of law, administrative tribunals, or executive action. Most treaties on economic cooperation, however, require that only judicial remedies be exhausted. The Treaty of Economic Cooperation between the United States and Ireland [June 28, 1948, United States–Ireland, 62(2) Stat. 2407, 2416, T.I.A.S. No. 1788, at 12] states, for example:

> It is further understood that neither Government will espouse a claim pursuant to this Article until its national has exhausted the remedies available to him in the *administrative tribunal and judicial tribunals* of the country in which the claim arose.

The rule is relevant only in cases of international claims arising from disputes involving individuals or corporations and not to direct state-to-state claims because a state cannot be said to have "local" remedies to exhaust in another state for an international claim. It should be noted, however, that claims brought by states on behalf of individuals or corporations rarely come before international tribunals.

Nations may suspend or eliminate by treaty the requirement that local remedies be exhausted. The requirement may be dispensed with generally or only in specified circumstances. A home nation will suspend the exhaustion rule when denial of justice has occurred. The concept of denial includes the whole area of state responsibility toward foreign nationals and will be applied to all types of wrongful conduct on the part of a host state toward foreign nationals. For example, a denial of justice takes place when a foreign national is denied access to local courts or has been subjected to inadequate procedures or unjust decisions.

The exhaustion rule protects the interests of both the foreign national and a host state. By respecting the sovereignty of states and the primacy of national jurisdiction in international disputes, the rule permits states the flexibility necessary to regulate their internal affairs. At the same time, the rule requires states to recognize their international responsibility to offer justice to foreign nationals. Thus, the rule protects the interests of the multinational by promising either effective local remedies or a remedy in an international forum.

Comity

Comity is the recognition that one nation extends within its jurisdiction to the legislative, executive, or judicial acts of another nation. The extension of comity is a voluntary decision of the state, not an act required by international law. It is a decision that is influenced by politics, courtesy, and good faith; hence, it is not a rule of law but one of practice, convenience, and expediency. Although comity is more than a mere accommodation, it is still discretionary; it can be viewed as a nation's expression of an understanding of the needs of the international system and the rights of persons protected by its own laws.

Letters Rogatory

Letters rogatory are the official medium through which evidence is obtained by one country, speaking through its courts, from another country, acting through its courts to assist in the resolution of a dispute. To obtain letters rogatory, a U.S. lawyer petitions the district court where an action is pending for the issuance of the letters to the appropriate judicial authority in the foreign country. The letters rogatory first convey the official greetings of the President of the United States to the requisite judicial authority in the foreign country; for example:

> In this case here at issue, the form of the letters rogatory . . . is made the medium of conveying the official greetings of his Excellency, the President of the United States, to the Supreme Court, Russian Soviet Federated Socialist Republic, Moscow, U.S.S.R., and of giving assurance to said court that we shall be pleased to do the same for you in a similar case, when required. (*Tiedman* v. *The Signe*, 37 F. Supp. 920 (1941))

The letter rogatory then requests, under the authority of the named court, certain evidence necessary for the purpose of discovery or for use as evidence in the action being taken in the U.S. court; for example:

. . . in the furtherance of justice you will by the proper and usual service of process cause the witness hereinabove named . . . to appear before the consul of the United States to give the requested evidence. (*R.C.A.* v. *Rouland Corporation and Another*, (1956) 1 Q.B. 618)

As a rule, foreign courts will, by reason of comity, grant the request for judicial assistance. However, if national interests are involved or the request is a "fishing expedition" for possible evidence, it may be denied.

LITIGATION

The litigation of international disputes involves the application of both foreign and international law by a domestic court. Investors look to the courts of the host country, their home country, or possibly even a third country in situations that are serious enough to require litigation.

Domestic courts often are called upon to choose between a solution based upon a domestic public policy that serves the interests of their nation or one based upon an international public policy that serves the common interests of the "law of nations." To accomplish this, the domestic court must be able to understand the structure of world society and its need for resolutions of disputes that are both orderly and have the fewest possible ramifications. In this way a domestic court will be able to give "binding force and effect to principles of international law."

Private International Law

Private international law comes into play whenever a domestic court is called upon to resolve a contractual controversy that involves a foreign element (see Chapter 1). Private international law operates only when this element is present and has as its object: (1) to prescribe the conditions under which a particular domestic court may hear such a suit; (2) to determine the particular system of law by which the rights of the parties must be decided; and (3) to specify the circumstances in which a foreign judgment can be recognized or enforced.

Private international law is applied whenever the issue before the court affects part of an international contract and is connected with a foreign legal system so as to necessitate a resort to that system. For example, a promise made by a British citizen in Italy and to be performed there, if valid and enforceable by Italian law, would not be unenforceable by an English court merely because the promise was unsupported by consideration. In a case like this, the English court would select appropriate rules from Italian law to govern the resolution of the controversy.

Private international law is not a separate branch of law, like contract law. It is, however, a separate and distinct unit within a domestic legal system, agreed to by the parties to a sales transaction, and it is not the same in all cases or in all nations. For example, in Great Britain the validity of a contract is determined by the laws of the legal system that has the closest connection to the agreement; whereas in the United States the law of the place where the contract was made or the law of the place of performance governs.

Jurisdiction

Jurisdiction is the capacity of a nation to prescribe a course of conduct for its citizens and also to enforce a rule of law on its citizens. In order to enforce any legal rule, both jurisdiction to prescribe and jurisdiction to enforce that rule must be present.

When an individual served with a notice of action is a foreign subject on foreign soil, this service presents no jurisdictional problems. The serving by a governmental agency of a notice of the pendency of an action gives the recipient information upon which to make a decision whether to act. It prescribes a court of conduct for the person. When compulsory process is served, however, the act of service is an exercise of one nation's sovereignty within the territory of another and is a violation of international law. A notice of compulsory process orders a witness to do something and threatens sanctions for not complying. For example, when the Federal Trade Commission serves a complaint upon a person, the purpose of service is primarily notice, rather than compulsion. However, when he or she is served with a copy of the complaint and the proposed order, the person has the choice of meeting with the commission to negotiate a consent order or of proceeding to litigation. In this situation, the coercive power of the courts is brought directly to bear upon the person. Informational service of process from the United States to a foreign country minimizes the imposition upon local authority caused by the action. However, compulsory subpoena service, without warning to the local officials and without an initial request for or prior resort to established channels of international judicial assistance, is regarded as intrusive. Not only does it represent a deliberate bypassing of local authority but it also allows foreign judicial sanctions for non-compliance to be imposed if a foreign citizen is unwilling to comply with the directives.

Courts sometimes weigh the existence of jurisdictional power against the wisdom of exercising it. For example, the court weighs the interests of the United States in obtaining evidence against the interests of a foreign government. Thus, in a situation where production of evidence would violate the criminal laws of the foreign nation, U.S. courts may not order it, because this would be unfair to the party charged and the enforcement of such an order would affect relationships between the nations.

The United States is a frequent offender of other nations' jurisdictional rights and perhaps it should take a less parochial attitude toward foreign interests. The U.S. Supreme Court, in *M/S Bremen* v. *Zapata Off-Shore Company*, 407 U.S. 1 (1972), encouraged a broader view:

> The expansion of American business and industry will hardly be encouraged if, notwithstanding solemn contracts, we insist on a parochial concept that all disputes must be resolved under our laws and in our courts. . . . We cannot have trade and commerce in world markets in international waters exclusively on our terms, governed by our laws and resolved in our courts.

In practice, however, U.S. courts have paid little more than lip service to the *Zapata* language and have not sufficiently focused upon or understood foreign interests.

Substance and Procedure

In private legal action a distinction is made between substance and procedure, between right and remedy. The substantive rights of the parties in international disputes may be governed by a foreign law, but procedural matters are governed by the law of the forum. For example, a person who resorts to a French court for the purpose of enforcing a foreign claim against a French citizen cannot expect to occupy a different procedural position from that of a domestic litigant. A litigant in France must take the law of procedure as he or she finds it. An individual cannot, by virtue of some rule in his or her own country, enjoy greater advantages than other litigants. At the same time, the foreign litigant must not be deprived of any advantages that French law may confer upon a French litigant in the case.

The distinction between substance and procedure is made for the convenience of the court. When faced with a conflict of laws, the court is bound to apply the *lex causae*, but it cannot be expected to also import all the relevant rules of the foreign law. To apply the foreign rules of procedure would be inconvenient and impractical. It is, however, general international policy for domestic courts to apply foreign substantive law whenever possible. The court where the action is brought determines, according to its own law, whether a matter is one of substance or procedure. As a rule, procedure involves those steps that any person must take in order to bring an action before a proper court. The following are some of the major factors that are generally classified as procedural when a conflict of laws occurs:

> actionability of the claim
>
> identity of the proper parties to the litigation
>
> admissibility of evidence
>
> relative priority of protected interests
>
> set-off
>
> the nature and extent of the remedy
>
> methods of enforcing judgment
>
> right to appeal

Preparing for Trial

The United States has established a more elaborate system of discovering facts and of simplifying matters in advance of trial than have other nations. Discovery procedures in the United States reduce the secrecy factor by allowing each party access to the other's witnesses and documents, subject, of course, to certain safeguards. During the course of a trial involving a foreign party, the parties may need evidence, documentary or personal, available only in other countries and will therefore ask a foreign court for assistance in obtaining it. This raises some problems because among legal systems the concepts of judicial procedure differs widely, the rules of evidence are interpreted differently, and protected interests are given different priorities. Some legal systems stress the oral presentation of evidence by witnesses, with the opportunity for cross-examination to determine the truth. Other systems place a great deal of weight on the accuracy of documentation as evidence. There are countries where judges have the duty to develop the evidence by determining the truthfulness of the witnesses; in other countries attorneys have that responsibility.

All legal systems protect certain types of records and preclude some types of oral testimony. The protected interests usually include official secrets, confidential relationships, and bank records. Which interests are protected varies from nation to nation as does the degree of reciprocity nations are willing to exercise. Many nations , however, place confidentiality above a foreign court's search for the truth. Foreign secrecy laws, for example, may carry penal sanctions for disclosure of confidential information. Thus, an American discovery order requiring confidential information that is subject to the foreign law would create hardship for the party having knowledge of the information.

The Enforcement of Foreign Judgments

When a plaintiff obtains a judgment in a court of a foreign country, he or she sometimes finds that the defendant has insufficient assets to satisfy the judgment. If the defendant has property in other countries, it becomes important to know whether those countries will recognize and enforce a foreign judgment. In fact, courts have long recognized and enforced foreign judgments in certain circumstances. For example, when a judgment determines the status of persons, such as marital status, it calls for no more than recognition and no question of enforcement arises. However, a foreign judgment for a definite sum of money imposes a legal obligation on the defendant, which requires enforcement. Thus, there is a significant difference between enforcement and recognition. Enforcement requires the aid of the legal system to establish the plaintiff's foreign judgment, whereas recognition merely requires the acceptance of a status, such as a foreign divorce decree.

A successful plaintiff who has obtain a foreign judgment has the choice of suing again in the domestic court on the original cause of action or of bringing suit on the basis of the foreign judgment. In the first instance, the domestic court will examine the merits of the case, while in the latter it will only do so under exceptional circumstances. Two conditions must be satisfied for foreign judgments to be enforced: (1) the judgment must have been given by a court of competent jurisdiction; (2) the judgment must be final and conclusive. Despite the fact that foreign judgments are usually conclusive, there are some defenses that can be raised to an action brought to enforce them. These defenses are based on claims of fraud, issues of public policy, and the injustice of the decision.

Tort Laws and U.S. Business

The level of tort liability on U.S. firms doing business abroad is a large burden. It raises the price of U.S. goods and services produced either in the United States or overseas. Numerous aircraft and drug companies, for example, have been sued in this country for products sold and, in some instances, even manufactured and licensed abroad. The U.S. tort system is, by far, the world's most generous for victorious plaintiffs. The reasons for such high levels of liability in our legal system can be found in its substantive rules (such as strict liability); procedural rules (such as discovery) that facilitate litigation; measures of damages (such as pain and suffering and punitive damages), which increase the amount of a potential judgment; juries that value human life and suffering more highly than do those in other countries; and contingency fee arrangements, illegal everywhere else in the world, that allow plaintiffs' lawyers to increase the costs of litigation.

Products differ, of course, in the amount of damage they can cause and, thus, in the amount their price is raised to make provision for potential lawsuits. For some products, such as a bar of soap, the degree of risk is quite small, and the corresponding rise in price minimal. But for other products, such as earth-moving machinery, incorporating the cost of liability can be enough to cause a loss of a substantial market share.

ARBITRATION

Over the years, individuals and business firms have sought alternative methods for settling international business disputes. Recent developments have encouraged wider use of arbitration as the principal alternative to litigation. Domestic courts are increasingly willing to recognize and enforce international arbitration agreements and awards granted in other countries. The decision in *Scherk* v. *Alberto-Culver Company*, 417 U.S. 506 (1974), expressed the view of the United States: "A parochial refusal by the courts of one country to enforce an international arbitration agreement would not only frustrate the purposes, but it would invite unseemly and mutually destructive jockeying by the parties to secure tactical litigation advantages." Arbitration is not recognized in Japan, however, because it suggests to the Japanese that resolution of a dispute will be entrusted to an outsider of the dispute. The Japanese wish to preserve the harmonious relationship arrived at by the parties concerned during negotiation of the contract, a relationship that would be disrupted by even the potential admission of an outsider.

Commercial arbitration allows the parties to agree in advance on the rules for resolving their trade disputes and for dispute settlement to occur in a neutral forum. Their agreement to arbitrate should be in writing and it should provide a relatively quick and simple mechanism for resolving "interpretive" differences that might arise and suggest possible remedies. For example, the word *reasonable* does not exist in the Russian language. The concept "reasonable" translates as *adequate*, and if the word *reasonable* is used in a contract, U.S. negotiators would be at a disadvantage because they accept the so-called reasonable standard of law.

Statutes and Treaties on Arbitration

The existence of an arbitration statute in every state in the United States is testimony to the widening use of arbitration. In addition, the United States Arbitration Act and a host of treaties on arbitration, including treaties of friendship, commerce, and navigation, the multinational treaty on arbitration in the New York Convention of 1958, and the Inter-American Arbitration Convention of 1975, are now in force. The New York Convention on the Recognition and Enforcement of Foreign Arbitral Awards, ratified by over sixty countries and in force in the United States since 1970, is a multilateral treaty on enforcement of foreign arbitral awards. It provides for the recognition of arbitral agreements, and it prevents courts from adjudicating disputes that the parties have agreed to arbitrate. Thus, the arbitral process has been given a greater degree of uniformity and credibility than it once had.

The Arbitration Agreement

International arbitration encompasses a number of rules that may differ from case to case according to the choice of the institutional framework for arbitration or to the rules agreed upon by the parties. There are a number of rules and practices, however, that are common to all international arbitration situations.

The Arbitration Clause

Two basic points must be settled by each party to an agreement: (1) the content of the arbitration clause, and (2) the procedure for selecting the arbitrators. These points are settled before a dispute arises, although the selection of the actual arbitrator is done in most cases when a dispute becomes apparent. The arbitration clause usually is not drafted to meet a specific dispute situation because the exact nature of a dispute cannot be determined ahead of time. This does not relieve the parties from making an effort to achieve clarity and completeness in the drafting of the clause, however, because the clause must state clearly what the scope of the potential arbitration will be, even the language in which the arbitration is to be conducted. Nor can some definition of the nature of potential disputes be avoided. Obviously, due to the variety of transactions, no definition can cover all situations, but some areas are subject to prior agreement between the parties. The arbitration clause must also address differences stemming from legal relationships, whether contractual or not, that are considered commercial. The clause must, therefore, take into account the laws governing arbitration in the countries concerned and whether these countries are contracting parties to relevant arbitration treaties, as well as the legal effect of future accession by these countries to one or more of those treaties.

The Choice of Law.   An important point in an arbitration clause is the choice of substantive as well as of procedural law to govern the arbitration. Each side will want the law of its own country to govern the contract and arbitration; the choice of a third country's law is the usual compromise. In loan agreements, the law of an important financial center, such as New York or London, would be considered; whereas in investment agreements, the law of the host country is often chosen as the controlling law.

The Choice of Forum.   The arbitration clause will provide for arbitration within a preexisting institutional framework or arbitration not related to a preexisting institutional framework, or *ad hoc* arbitration. A number of forums exist for institutionalized arbitration, and over the years some fairly uniform and accepted rules have evolved for conducting such proceedings. The London Court of Arbitration, established in 1892 for the purpose of dealing with private commercial transactions, is one such forum, and others are available in Geneva, New York, Paris, and Stockholm. Refusal of recognition and enforcement of the award is less likely to occur if the proceedings have been conducted at one of the major arbitration centers. In 1976, the United Nations Commission on Trade Law issued its model international commercial arbitration rules (UNCITRAL) in an effort to establish some sort of uniformity. As a model, these rules are intended for worldwide adoption. The London Court of Arbitration and the Stockholm Chamber of Commerce have shown a willingness to work with these rules.

One of the purposes of choosing a forum for arbitration is to select a legal system that subjects the proceedings to a minimal amount of judicial interference prior to, during, and afterwards. In both England and France, arbitration laws offer opportunities for interference by the local courts. American lawyers dislike the narrow scope of the discovery procedures in arbitration and the arbitrator's ability to compel the production of documentary evidence.

Selection of the Arbitrators. Two factors are considered when selecting arbitrators for *ad hoc* arbitration: the procedure for appointment and the procedures to be observed for challenging an arbitrator. Generally, two arbitrators, one appointed by each party, are agreed upon. A third arbitrator may also be selected by the parties or by agreement of the two arbitrators appointed by the parties.

The Arbitrator's Authority

The private resolution of international disputes raises the question of the source of the arbitrator's authority to render a binding award. A multinational enterprise that submits a dispute to arbitration may later regret having abandoned a recourse to the courts. Legal systems, therefore, must legitimize the arbitrator's authority.

The country where the award is made generally will impose conditions on arbitral authority in the form of mandatory procedural rules to be followed in the proceedings. These local norms — commonly known as the *lex loci arbitri* — are established to ensure legally correct results, to safeguard fundamental fairness, and to free the proceedings from any constraints. The mandatory rules prohibit arbitration of disputes involving sensitive public interests, such as the protection of investors in corporate securities or contracts with state agencies. Some require arbitrators to state the reasons for their awards or provide for the removal of arbitrators who are inept or unfair. English judges traditionally have given the *lex loci arbitri* more weight than the French or American courts. One English decision held that the selection of London as a *situs* for arbitration implied that English substantive law governed the issue of contract damages. In contrast, American and French decisions have minimized the influence of the law of the place of arbitration.

A legal system that subjects international arbitration to its judicial control might limit its inquiry to ascertaining the award's basic integrity; for example, the arbitrator's impartiality. Or, the courts might concern themselves only with the legal merits of the dispute. The extent of judicial control will depend upon whether it is more important that an arbitral award be correct or that it be final. Judicial control over the substantive legal issues of an international arbitration should likewise be minimal. Parties to the dispute should have the privacy for which they bargained. In addition, arbitrators should be free from the threat of being overruled because of errors in their analysis so that reasoned awards will be rendered more frequently, thereby contributing to the development of arbitral legal principles.

By allowing an award rendered on its territory to become binding, a state facilitates enforcement of an award. However, it should also provide a mechanism for challenging any procedural deficiencies in the making of an award. Otherwise, the losing party might challenge the award in each of the many states where the award might be enforced against its property. The contesting party should have an opportunity to expose procedural irregularities at the place of the arbitration.

SUMMARY

An international commercial dispute may require resolution by a court within the host country, by a court within the home country, or by a court within a third country. Wherever the dispute is resolved, time will be consumed and expenses incurred, and difficulties may arise in obtaining the necessary persons or documents required by the procedural rules of the appropriate forum. And the question arises of whether the decision will be legally correct or politically correct.

The uncertainty of litigation and of the enforcement of the judgment by other courts has made arbitration a preferred method of resolving international commercial disputes. Submission to arbitration is accomplished in advance of a dispute by an agreement to an arbitration clause within a contract. Choice of law and choice of forum clauses allow the parties to set their own rules to resolve commercial disputes and to avoid the surprises of litigation. In addition to other treaties, the New York Convention on the Recognition and Enforcement of Foreign Arbitral Awards encourages international recognition and enforcement of arbitration agreements and awards.

SUGGESTED CASE READINGS

Frummer v. *Hilton Hotels International Inc.*, 227 N.E.2d 851 (1967).

Nielson v. *Secretary of Treasury*, 424 F.2d 833 (1970).

R.C.A. v. *Rouland Corp. and Another*, (1956) 1 Q.B. 618.

U.S. v. *First National City Banks*, 396 F.2d 897 (1968).

Hilton et. al. v. *Guyot et. al.*, 159 U.S. 113 (1895).

Oregon-Pacific Forest Products Corp. v. *Welsh Panel Co.*, 248 F. Supp. 903 (1965).

DISCUSSION QUESTIONS

1. What are the two basic disputes that may arise in international trade agreements?
2. What doubts are raised in domestic courts with regard to the validity of an international judicial decision?
3. Explain the international principle of comity in international litigation.
4. Should arbitration by subject to judicial review?
5. Will sovereign immunity ever be a factor in an arbitration proceeding?
6. Is there a public policy defense against the enforcement of arbitral awards?

EPILOGUE

There is little doubt that there are international dimensions of the legal environment for business. Multinational firms conduct their commercial activities in the many nations that are part of world society. They move goods, people, and technological know-how all over the globe in an effort to bring about an optimal allocation of their capital, personnel, and other resources. At the same time, nations face the challenge of making a rational use of their limited resources to meet their national priorities.

A desire for prosperity and a better life for their citizens makes the nations of the world competitors for available foreign investment. In order to facilitate this type of activity, nations make "agreements" with each other. In political and economic terms, some of these nations are equal and some are unequal. International law does not presume that sovereign nations are equal in world power and status. As competitors for foreign investment, each nation's concept of sovereignty affects the world business climate. Some newer nations, jealous of their sovereign power, are reluctant to grant complete freedom to the foreign investor. Most investors try to avoid these uncertainties of national policy. Other nations, eager to develop national resources, grant complete freedom to the foreign investor.

Like nations, the multinational enterprise also may have conflicting goals. At the outset, it must please its owners by increasing profits. To accomplish this, it must offer consumers a better product. The situation is complicated, however, by the requirement that the multinational aid its host in achieving national goals. Business policy must, therefore, include being a good citizen by paying taxes, obeying local laws, and gradually blending products, organization, and people into the local environment. To do otherwise will invite the host to exercise more control over its business activities. In some situations, failure to be a good citizen results in loss of the firm's asserts due to a taking by the host government.

The potential for corporate and national conflict has led to the development of alternative methods for doing business in the world marketplace. Licensing and joint ventures are safer ways of conducting business than investing locally. And local participation in such arrangements, either on a majority or minority basis, is more acceptable to the parent firm.

The day of a true world community, regulated by international rules, has not yet arrived. Perfect harmony between multinational enterprises and host governments is also an ideal yet to be fully realized. But the words of Professor T. O. Elias, former Chief Justice of Nigeria and now a judge of the International Court of Justice at the Hague, may be prophetic:

> The trust is that modern international law, for all its lack of enforceability, has developed and will continue to develop to meet the constantly changing needs of the world of today and of tomorrow, a world of growing interdependence and indivisibility that is also committed to the achievement of peace and happiness for all mankind.

Index